The Boomer Guide to Finding True Love Online

by Ken Solin

First Edition 2014

ISBN 10: 1-941957-09-9   ISBN 13: 978-1-941957-09-7

21ST CENTURY
LION BOOKS

21st Century Lion Books
P.O. Box 669238
Pompano Beach, FL 33066
www.globallionmanagement.com

To Sarah, for her love and patience.

"Dating after 50 has its own issues and needs its own advice. Ken Solin makes sure that part of that advice includes the male perspective – both in order to help women to understand men better when they return to dating and also to help men understand the process, their emotions, and their own strategies better. This is an extremely useful addition to the dating literature for mature men and women." – Pepper Schwartz PhD, author *Dating after 50 for Dummies* (Wiley, 2014), *AARP* love, sex and relationship Ambassador

The Boomer Guide to Finding True Love Online

Table of Contents

Preface

Who Are Boomers?

Technically, a boomer was born after January 1, 1946 and before 1964. Boomers turned America's attitudes about social justice and political issues upside down. We were the sex, drugs, and rock and roll generation and our motto, "the status quo has got to go," reflected our passion for social and political change. We decided no one over thirty could be trusted, designating the majority of Americans, suspect. Young men wore their hair long, grew beards, pasted peace symbols on their T-shirts, cars, and anywhere else a sticker could be affixed, and felt that free love was a young man's rite of passage. Young women dressed in long denim skirts made from old jeans, tie-dye tank tops, and considered sex in the same free love manner as men. Our nearly manic drive to be different than previous generations fueled our art, music, politics, humor, sexuality, and more. Sometimes, we used psychedelic drugs and marijuana to inspire our efforts in those arenas.

A Force To Be Reckoned With

We toppled a President when he ignored our outrage, shouting, "Hey hey LBJ, how many kids did you kill today," loud enough for Lyndon Johnson to hear in his White House bedroom. His ill fated war aside, he did muscle the Civil Rights Act and Medicare through Congress.

We were a powerful force to reckon with; we demonstrated, and sometimes, when we didn't get what we wanted, we rioted. We mourned the Kennedy brothers and Martin Luther King, whose deaths signaled the end of one political era and the beginning of another. We rejected the old guard and they feared us; we enjoyed that sense of power. We weren't all hippies, but most of us appreciated the changes the Hippy Movement stood for.

Then and Now

There's a world of difference between what boomers wanted from relationships in the 60s and 70s and what most of us want now. In the 60s and into the 70s we shed our romantic partners like soiled T-shirts, frequently with the same amount of regret. We graduated from college or went into the trades. We got married, had children, and tried to create families different than those we grew up in. Half of us got divorced, which presented boomers with a brand new set of problems, including a new type of painful emotional experience, an experience that we also felt in our wallets. Some of us still carry the emotional fallout from those divorces in our psyches, resulting in a wariness and lack of trust between the genders. We stung each other deeply, and that left many of us hesitant and mistrustful about relationships.

Contrary to what a small number of boomer guys wistfully fantasize about, the free love that we practiced way back when, isn't remotely the model for boomer dating today. Most of us have figured out that sex alone can't carry a relationship. After too many sexually fueled rocket-rides, boomers want more than a lover; they want a real partnership. Technology enables us to find potential partners while sitting at home and surfing the Internet. This is a technical challenge for a few, but senior dating sites are making online dating easier by requiring minimal technical skills.

Magic Happens

The notion that a boomer should ever consider settling, in terms of choosing a partner, is totally misguided. If someone tells you that you're being picky, that's actually good, because picky should be your absolute minimum standard. What's the gold standard? Magic. Yes, magic can happen, and if you don't believe it, then you just haven't experienced it yet. Call it the thunderbolt, magic, or whatever name you choose, it's real and it can happen to you if you're open to it and know how to recognize it.

Magic and infatuation are not the same. Infatuation is exciting, but temporary. Magic is intense and lasts. When I kissed my partner Sarah good-bye at the end of our first date I felt the magic racing through my entire body. It was a soft, gentle kiss, but it felt electric, and it wasn't just lust. I felt it in my heart as well as my body. It was obvious that something powerful was happening. We hugged after that kiss and parted shortly after. We both felt something wonderful might be happening, and that whatever it was might carry with it the possibility of a relationship. We didn't want to become sexual until we felt certain it was as special as it seemed. We needed some space to process these strong, nascent feelings. Nearly two years later I still feel that magic when we get together, and when we make love it's at a level that I describe in the book as TBSI, the best sex imaginable. Don't sell magic short, and for heaven's sake, don't think it can't happen to you. It just takes patience, stamina, and a little luck.

Partners, Not Rocket Riders

What seems clear from the thousands of single boomers I've heard from is that few of us want to spend the rest of our lives alone. It's that desire not to remain solo that propels us to seek partners. Unlike the 60s and 70s when we didn't pay much attention to our dates' inner qualities, we're no longer willing to cut our candidates for partners much slack. An evolved emotional sensibility is prized. Women in particular, focus on partnering with men who have done some amount of inner work and are capable of carrying their weight in a relationship. We're so worried about not making any more bad choices that dating can make us feel anxious and even fearful.

The 60s are over for the great majority of boomers and I can't recall one woman I dated ever mentioning the 60s, with the exception of the music. Most of us have gladly moved beyond that period, and few of us remain stuck in that psychedelic culture, Deadheads notwithstanding. We're more interested in what's happening in our lives today than in the past, and we aren't aging mentally or physically as quickly as our parents.

Like many guys of my generation I decided to try online dating several years ago because I couldn't imagine a richer source of boomer women to date. While I found online dating amazingly helpful, it's a maze for lots of boomers. Online dating remains out of reach for some simply because it involves computers. Others insist that there aren't any good prospects online after briefly trying it out. Some simply give up, insisting they'll just bump into the loves of their lives at the supermarket. The computer issue is fairly easily resolved, and there are, in fact, a plethora of good relationship prospects online. It's incredibly naïve to believe you'll bump into your life partner, who has all the qualities you require, at the supermarket or anywhere else. That only happens in the movies. You need to be proactive.

In the past decade I became a Dating Expert for several online magazines. A short list includes *AARP, The Huffington Post, About.com,* and *Maria Shriver.* This book is based on my extensive dating experience and the dating experiences of tens of thousands of readers who have commented on my articles. I dated online from its inception, which gives me a historical perspective. I struggled with the same online dating issues as other boomers. I had enormous stamina and determination, both of which helped develop proficient computer skills to make online dating viable.

Online Dating Works

I met my sweetheart online by using the guidelines I detail in this book. I figured out how to maximize online dating and used that information as my primary dating resource. My partner and I had effectively ignored each other on the same website for a year until I finally discovered her by using the methodologies I offer in *The Boomer Guide to Finding True Love Online.* The same qualities I used to identify Sarah as a potential partner have enabled us to deepen our intimacy. Will the information in this book, work for every single boomer man and woman? Yes, it absolutely can. Most boomers date for the same reason, to meet their life partners. *The Boomer Guide to Finding True Love* takes most of the sting out of online dating by offering clear, experiential information gleaned from thousands of men and women, all looking for a lasting relationship.

There wouldn't be any need for *The Boomer Guide to Finding True Love Online* if boomers just wanted to find a date. But boomers want much more than a date. They want their next, first date to be their last, first date. This guide fills a huge void of quality online boomer dating information.

Tricks and gimmicks typically found in dating books are useless for boomers. Instead, *The Boomer Guide to Finding True Love Online* offers real-life solutions boomer men and women can relate to and utilize. Dating questions, such as why boomer men and women are perfect for each other, why emotional honesty is critical, and what it means to date smart, are answered in detail. Neither gender has a lock on appropriate dating behavior and both will benefit from the information in this book.

My Guiding Light

When I began writing a book steeped in boomer men's and women's interactive behavior, the frame of reference that kept popping into my head were the lessons I'd learned over a quarter century with other men. So much of what I know about relationships as they relate to being an emotionally empowered man, developed from eight men sharing our stories. What worked and what didn't work for us, and for the women we were in relationships with, was always open for discussion.

Decades after we began meeting, the issue that still comes up most often is relationships. While we all want to get it right with women and we're equally concerned about retaining our strong sense of manhood. There was little consensus regarding what a strong guy was supposed to look like when we first met. The points of view ranged from super macho to quasi-feminine, and the gap was wide enough to drive an eighteen-wheeler through.

The dialogue about what comprised manhood became so heated at times that anger, shouting, and even threats of violence were grist for the mill. I'd grown up in a violent home in a rough town, so anger and threats of violence seemed like normal male behavior to me. Other men felt differently, however, and some threatened to leave the group if we couldn't find common ground. The split led me to call Sam Keane, author or *Fire in the Belly* and a men's group advocate, for advice. His terse comment explained everything about our process. "You're a men's group, aren't you?" We forged on and in time the anger diminished as eight guys learned how to speak from their hearts and not just their heads. The bonus was that our wives and girlfriends also benefited from our ability to articulate our feelings in a strong and in control manner.

It was our ability to identify, control, and share our emotions with everyone around us that empowered us. We'd met initially to achieve a common goal, which was to become better men, and it was the strength derived from the work we did together that enabled each of us to realize his highest sense of manhood. I routinely resolve relationship issues with my partner Sarah because of the lessons I learned with other men. Sometimes it can be clumsy, but it's never impossible.

Boomer women write that some boomer guys they've met exhibited incredibly dysfunctional dating behavior, and that they wished men had a better dating roadmap. *The Boomer Guide to Finding True Love Online* puts boomer men on a path toward changing that without affecting men's spirits or demeaning their manhood. Women play an equally important role in this dialogue, and I detail what their part in this process looks like. Relationship issues are inevitable and they can't be resolved if only one person has the requisite skills. For the vast majority of boomers this isn't innate ability, but rather learned behavior.

Boomer women will find all the information they need to identify the right guys to date. I share what to look for inside a man in specific and quantifiable terms, and I explain what minimal relationship skills he should have. The outside is chemistry, and that's different for everyone. I also share how boomers sometimes sabotage their dating efforts by typecasting their dates. I'm a big fan of boomer women and I dated them exclusively until I met my boomer partner Sarah. What I find fascinating is that she doesn't look or behave at all like the women I dated previously. That only became possible when I stopped typecasting my dates. I've gleaned further information through coaching men and women about dating. When women's hearts become hardened to the dating process after several painful experiences, the only way to get onto a positive dating path again is to soften their hearts and become emotionally open again. Of course, the same is true for men who often become emotionally distant after getting their hearts broken to ward off intimacy and the pain they worry will inevitably follow.

I point out to the myriad reasons why boomer women are the perfect dates and partners for boomer men. I explain why this is true and also what men should look for in a woman. I detail what appropriate dating behavior looks like for boomer men and women and I urge both to learn how to hold their own in the emotional dating and relationship arenas. Men are generally physically stronger than women, but their emotional strength often lags behind that of women. I share how boomer men and women can effectively put themselves on a path to create harmony instead of conflict.

Why Boomers Make Perfect Partners—for Each Other

The goal of *The Boomer Guide to Finding True Love Online* is to bring boomer men and women together again so we can enjoy the level of camaraderie we did when we were younger. Sure, our lives have changed quite a lot since then, but our commonality of interests and goals is still far greater than our differences. Boomers can be ideal partners for each other once they bridge the gap that's primarily about a mutual lack of trust. My mentor was absolutely right about relationships when he opined, "Where there's no trust, there's no love."

Ask any boomer to imagine what qualities and characteristics a perfect partner would need to have to meet their requirements. Most list passion, friendship, a peer, a sense of humor, attractiveness, and emotional availability. When asked where they hope to find this person, few seem to know where to look. The answer is staring right at boomer men and women. It's other boomers, most of whom have these qualities, and more, in abundance. I've written extensively about why boomer men and women are perfect for each other and *The Boomer Guide to Finding True Love Online* explains the many reasons why. Successful online dating depends on several factors, but the most important is narrowing the field of candidates by focusing solely on other boomers.

You Can't Please Everyone

If I wrote a book about boomer dating to please everyone, I wouldn't please anyone. While there are few absolute truths regarding boomer dating, there are numerous areas of gender agreement and disagreement that are nearly universal in sentiment. I deliberated whether or not to write extensively about the emotional aspect of boomer dating. In the end, I realized that it's a major aspect of it that begged to be addressed. The emotional component of boomer dating is at the root of the gender conflict, which I was surprised to discover when I began dating again after a divorce. The thousands of comments my dating articles have received in *The Huffington Post,* reflect wide ranging dating disappointments on both sides. My intention is to close the gender gap by addressing the conflict on a deeper level than dating tricks and gimmicks.

Foreword
by John Gray,
Author of the best-selling book
Men are From Mars, Women are from Venus

Ken's adherence to the *Men are From Mars, Women Are from Venus* philosophy of gender interaction is evident in his new boomer dating book, *The Boomer Guide to Finding True Love Online.* Ken details his online dating experiences along with those of thousands of readers who comment on his articles. His chapter on emotional honesty should be required reading for boomers before they date. The ability and willingness to express emotional truth is the foundation of a relationship, and it begins on the first date.

Ken applies his quarter century of experience working with men to boomer dating. His knowledge of male behavior is extensive and allows Ken to speak with authority. That women appreciate having Ken as a dating coach isn't surprising since he brings his experience with men into coaching, and he shares precisely what a woman should look for in a man. Ken also explains the issues that men need to address. When men and women use his hands on knowledge they can create a new and better boomer, dating paradigm.

I also enjoyed Ken's chapter in which he explains why boomer women are perfect partners for boomer men. He debunks all the myths about boomer men and women that have traditionally been problematic for choosing appropriate dates.

Ken's growth as a man, a friend, and a teacher has been remarkable to observe. He has his finger firmly on the pulse of the boomer dating community and he knows boomers are seeking a partner, and not just a date. His personal dating experiences are colorful and helpful, and Ken shares them in a refreshingly open and honest manner.

Ken met Sarah, his partner online and he shares the details of his relationship from the first date to the present. Ken offers information based on his dating experiences and he shares the details of his relationship with Sarah in a straightforward manner that's helpful for readers in their dating lives. He offers boomers creative ways to date, including many new methodologies not typically found in a boomer, dating book.

Chapter One:
Boomer Women

Eavesdropping

When I overhear a fellow boomer man talking about the perils of dating boomer women, I pay close attention. I'm not normally an eavesdropper, and I respect other people's privacy, but since I write about boomer dating for *AARP, The Huffington Post,* and *About.com* I'm always eager to learn anything that relates to the shifting sands of the boomer, dating paradigm. I feel heartened when I hear positive comments that suggest relations between boomer men and women are becoming less combative and more cordial. But, just as often, what I hear is one fellow warning another that dating boomer women is a mistake.

A Fan

It's only fair to admit upfront that I'm a huge fan of boomer women, and that my purpose in writing this chapter is to extol their virtues as superlative partners, lovers, and friends. In fact, I'm frankly puzzled why any man would eschew these amazing women in favor of a younger one. Sure, there's the obvious physical aspect of younger women, but when I stand naked in front of the mirror, the guy looking back is in pretty good shape, but he isn't the same guy he once was; it's easy for me to overlook a few wrinkles or extra pounds in a woman.

Our boomer bodies reflect a lifetime of experiences, and any physical imperfection is trumped by the joy of having made it this far. There's the fantasy and the reality when it comes to choosing a partner, and since the fantasy rarely lasts, I prefer the reality model. My goal is to point out the numerous reasons boomer men should consider dating boomer women. The only stipulation is that boomer women are our equals in every way, and in some instances, even our betters. For some men this idea doesn't sit well and may take some getting accustomed to. Listen up guys, because the quality of the last relationship you hope you'll ever be in is at stake. You can't afford to make any more mistakes.

Broad Brushes

Men partial to disparaging boomer women represent a small but vocal minority who seem to relish putting women down, and boomer women in particular. They make broad generalizations about boomer women. Two in particular sum up their points of view: "Boomer women are angry and bitter," and/or, "boomer women have too much baggage." What's typically behind this anti-boomer woman vitriol is very similar to what's behind the anti-woman hysteria that's been shouted from the rooftops by generally confused men for as long as I can remember.

It's more about women bashing than the truth, and the exact same comments they make about boomer women can just as easily be turned around by women and applied to them, and sometimes a small, but vocal, minority of women does turn those same comments around. School is out boomer guys. If you're dating with the purpose of meeting a life partner, behave like a serious adult, not a boy taunting the girls in the schoolyard.

Negative statements about angry, bitter women appear to emanate from two distinctly different reference points, both experiential. When I ask a man why he insists boomer women are bitter and angry, and I dig into his comments, I frequently discover that his attitude is actually a reflection of his feelings about his ex-wife or ex-girlfriend. Since I rarely hear anyone of either gender speak glowingly of an ex, the angry, bitter comments aren't surprising, but have nothing to do with the millions of women who don't happen to be that fellow's ex.

Making blanket statements about boomer women based on a relationship that ended badly, or a handful of dates, seems frivolous. They don't begin to make the case that boomer women are bitter or angry. Sour grapes is not a useful frame of reference when dating, and both men and women might want to consider letting go of their own angry, bitter attitudes before entering the boomer dating arena.

Boomer Women Rock

Boomer women have far more emotional, sexual, and intellectual depth than younger women. They've made their marks in the world and spent a lifetime perfecting them. That makes boomer women rich in the experiences that match boomer men far better than younger women. It's about the character these women developed through struggling in their lives as mothers, daughters, career women, and friends that makes them rewarding partners in intimate relationships.

Boomer women battled the system in place that prevented them from reaching the highest levels in business, politics, and education. The glass ceiling they broke through required a major effort that younger women never helped make happen, but whose benefits they enjoy. Boomer women had to deal with male bosses who controlled their destiny and prevented them from achieving their rightful places in the business world. This was a hard earned battle that younger women didn't wage, and while this doesn't mean young women are lesser women, they're not the same scrappy, gritty achievers as boomer women. Boomer women are being elected to congress, now comprise half of business graduate school enrollments, and half of medical and dental schools enrollments as well. A man who truly wants a peer life partner would do well to choose an age appropriate woman.

Men, Not Wallets

Women have achieved career successes that have translated into far-reaching economic gains, and it's this increased economic success that has given boomer women the ability to choose the men they date, based on reasons other than economic need. I remember dating in the 1970's and 1980's when a woman's economic status was shaky at best. Many single mothers worked and received some child support, but were still functionally broke. Economic hardship too often became the rationale that women considered in terms of what men to date. Today that's no longer the case, and unless you're a guy whose only appeal to women is the size of your bank account, the rest of us should be thrilled that women see us as men, not wallets. The fiscal decisions for dating decades ago are rapidly disappearing as women's salaries and opportunities continue to improve.

Parity

Perhaps the changing nature regarding which gender has the most money or the better paying job is causing some men to feel uncomfortable dating successful women, and perhaps they feel less desirable or in command. While there are likely women who are feeling their economic oats and only date men at their level of financial success or higher, my experience, and that of the myriad of men I'm in contact with, is that few women feel that way. The parity women generally seek doesn't have a price tag. It's more about emotional parity than financial equality, and if men want to be viewed as equals by women, that's where they might focus on stepping up their game.

Men who insist that women's rights have hurt them in dating and relationships reflect their unwillingness to look deeper into the reasons behind their own behavior. For some, there's a strong, inexplicable need to maintain what was the status quo before women's gains, even though that was a losing proposition for both genders. I have a vivid recollection of the 1960's Women's Movement. Like many men, I was confused by it at first, but I quickly realized that it worked in my favor too. I no longer had to be in charge or responsible for everything in a relationship.

The notion of having a woman as a true partner in a relationship grew on me quickly and became normal just as quickly. Few boomer women want to date a throwback stuck in a 1950's time warp as regards women; this is a non-starter for most. I'm not aware of any women who have any interest in meeting that guy. Boomer men have to choose between letting go of the past or remaining stuck in it.

Boomer Women's Muscles

Boomer women have strong character, and it was developed in part by standing shoulder to shoulder with their boomer brothers in the late sixties and early seventies, protesting a war they were neither being drafted for nor expected to fight. They stood with us in equal numbers because they cared about us enough to risk getting harassed, clubbed or tear-gassed. Boomer women did their part because they shared the same feelings and beliefs most young men held, that dying without purpose was incredibly stupid and wasteful. While some men heckled and hassled the protesters until the body count climbed into the tens of thousands with no end in sight, it was rare to see women protest the demonstrators. That alone speaks volumes about the ability boomer women had, and still have, to separate rhetoric from reality.

And More Muscle

Not long after the war ended, these same women took to the streets again, but this time to march for women's rights. I remember with some amount of shame, that unlike the war protests, women weren't joined by anything approximating an equal number of men when they marched to protest an unjust gender system. "What do these women want anyway?" That was the question men frequently asked when the Women's Movement began. Really, they didn't know? Women were being discriminated against in every aspect of American life, and there were men who actually couldn't grasp what the Women's Movement meant.

Boomer Women Hang Tough

Boomer women were as fiercely determined to end the gender gap as they'd been to end an unpopular war, and they stood strong while many men, and even some women, taunted them, particularly in the beginning. Just as there had been a fair amount of initial hostility toward the war protestors; there was a surprising amount of hostility from a vocal minority of men and women, who didn't seem to care a whit whether or not women were treated equally. It appears some men still feel similarly about women today. The difficulty for men decades ago was that there weren't any guidelines explaining how they should behave with "liberated" women, in dating or in relationships. Men came under a lot of fire. With nothing taken for granted and nothing off the table, men suffered from considerable confusion and anxiety about dating and relationships. Since the message today is that women want men to respect and treat them as equals, I can't fathom why any men still struggle to know what women want or how to behave with them.

Political Muscle

The Women's Movement was started by women, and for the most part, fought and won by women, which was no small feat. Every other social movement had found a modicum of support from those who weren't necessarily direct beneficiaries, but who became involved for moral reasons. And it's boomer women's political muscle that is so eagerly sought after now by politicians, because the new millennium reality is that women have to be courted separately from men to win national elections. Witness the last two presidential races, both won by the candidate the majority of women voters felt was more attuned with their sentiments. It was their votes that decided those elections. It's unlikely any male presidential candidate will ever again attempt to talk at women, instead of to them, if he hopes to win. It's that sense of determination and political muscle that's likely to make it possible for a woman candidate to run for President. If standing up for their rights, frequently alone, doesn't demonstrate boomer women's strength, courage, and determination, I can't imagine what might convince a man otherwise.

Overcoming Great Odds

Those men, who feel these same women are angry and bitter, might want to consider what these women had to achieve just to be treated fairly under the law. I struggle to imagine men in a similar situation, having to fight for equal treatment in the workplace, or elsewhere. There must be more I simply don't understand about men who bash boomer women, and perhaps some of my puzzlement is why some boomer guys aren't comfortable dating women strong enough to change laws and the popular culture.

Strong Support

Boomer men who disparage boomer women might want to rethink their angry, bitter judgment and see women as an incredible source of unrelenting support for them in relationships. Boomer women don't cut and run at the first sign of trouble, and that includes relationships. Their stamina for creating a scenario of fair play is highly developed and well honed. Boomer men should consider that quality extraordinarily desirable.

Authentic Friendships

Nearly every boomer woman I've ever known has had the same group of close girlfriends for decades, and sometimes, for a lifetime. The interpersonal skills required to maintain friendships for that long became highly developed over time. Knowing when it's appropriate to give, to push, or to compromise, being willing to admit fault, being unconditionally supportive, being loving no matter their differences, and maintaining those loving ties through marriages, divorces, deaths, sickness, and loneliness, are but some of the interpersonal skills boomer women bring to men in relationships. Boomer men should be thrilled to have the depth of friendship skills boomer women bring to relationships.

Unimaginable Devotion

I've been in a men's group for twenty-five years, and while there's little I wouldn't do for these men who are also my best friends, I'm not confident that how I feel about these guys is the same as how my partner Sarah feels about her best friends. She's sat with her friends through chemotherapy, comforted a best friend while dying, finds time to keep in constant contact with all her friends, and never fails to answer a friend's call for help. "I'm too busy," simply never applies. I've noticed her indomitable level of loyalty with her friends, and it has helped me appreciate her on a deeper level as a partner. She's always prepared to do whatever it takes to ease a friend's pain, including mine. I know only a few men who exhibit that depth of love and loyalty, including me. Sarah brings it all into our relationship. I've never felt so loved, supported, and cared for. Younger women may have terrific qualities, but they haven't achieved the potential for caring that boomer women have in abundance.

They Raised Our Children

Boomer women have raised our children, frequently as single mothers, and they've accomplished this Herculean task with a sense of unconditional love for their children. Many struggled financially and sacrificed to ensure their children's well being. I was a single father who raised an infant, a rare occurrence in the late 1960's. While it was exhausting to single parent a baby, and I had to invent my own childcare since it wasn't available back then, I never had to fight for equal pay in the workplace. I also never had any semblance of a social life during my single parent years. There were a few brief affairs, and lots of offers to be my son's mother, but none that interested me. I was twenty-three and I felt as if my life was going to be entirely devoted to my son as a single dad. I remarried six years after single parenting, while many single moms remain single for the duration of their children's childhoods. This takes a quiet kind of courage and devotion that men should respect and admire, especially since these moms raised our children and bring that strength into relationships.

Our Teachers

According to the Institute for Education Sciences, seventy-five percent of public school teachers are women, and fifty-six percent of those women are over forty. That many of these women are boomers, who have chosen a profession that won't make them wealthy, or even appreciated, is more than admirable. Some chose teaching because there weren't a plethora of opportunities in the male dominated business, medical, and science fields, while teaching was open to them. Whatever the reasons that compelled these women to teach our children, they deserve our respect and admiration. It's a thankless job that few are ever recognized for performing well, and fewer are compensated for appropriately. The high percentages of women teachers who fall into the boomer category have been at this task for many decades, and many are retiring now. We should all be grateful to them, and also concerned about the caliber of teachers replacing them. Boomer women have played a major, albeit quiet, role in creating healthy, smart adults, who also happen to be our children.

Yoko Ono Isn't Michelle Obama's Dress Designer

There's a generational culture gap between young and boomer women. I've never had to explain to my partner Sarah that Paul McCartney wasn't always a solo act, or that Jefferson Airplane didn't actually fly anywhere, at least on a jet. We laugh hysterically looking at old photos of the hippies we once were. Just after we began dating, Sarah showed me an old photo of her standing in front of a beat-up VW van with a giant peace symbol painted on its side door. That old van was so rusty its original color was impossible to determine. Sarah had more than a foot of brown frizzy hair that stood straight out like she'd stuck her finger in a light socket, a tie-dye T-shirt, bell bottom jeans, and high heeled, thigh-high boots. She was cute then, but I think she's more attractive now.

Boomer Women and Casual Sex

I haven't been a proponent of casual sex in a long while, but not for any moral reasons. My lack of enthusiasm for casual sex is related to the unsatisfying nature of sex with a stranger. It no longer intrigues me as it did decades ago; I rank it just above masturbation in terms of satisfaction. If I feel this way about casual sex, and based on the tens of thousands of comments after my boomer dating articles in *The Huffington Post,* other men mostly agree, it must be a minority of men whose misplaced hostility poisons the well. The women's universally supportive comments indicate most would prefer first-date sex enthusiasts go home and take care of their needs without their help. Boomer women aren't keen to share their bodies with strangers they don't know, trust, or feel safe with. That doesn't make them bitter or angry, it simply indicates their sense of self-respect is intact.

There's another aspect of casual sex that's both frightening and threatening: sexually transmitted diseases. While most STD's were fairly easily treated in the 1960's and 1970's, the HIV cloud puts an ominous tone on casual sex today, and particularly, unprotected sex. Bette Midler said it bluntly and succinctly: "A fuck ain't worth dying for."

For older guys who may be feeling anxious about sex with someone new anyway, by the time they've managed to open the condom package and put the condom on, thinking about why they're using a condom can wilt their intentions. Any man who expects a woman to even consider unprotected sex is idiotic in the extreme. No intelligent woman will feel remotely reassured by a man who insists he's HIV negative. Furthermore, men should be concerned about the physical and emotional health of a woman who agrees to have unprotected sex. Most couples wait until both partners feel emotionally ready to have sex, and then both get tested so that condoms aren't necessary. The notion of fumbling with condoms has become anathema to many boomers.

First Date Sex

Angry and bitter comments sometimes come from men who've been unsuccessful convincing boomer women to have first or second date sex with them. This frequently becomes their rationale for dating younger women who in reality may or may not feel casual sex is cool either. Is being turned down for casual sex a valid reason to disparage boomer women? When a man's unwanted initial sexual advances are rebuffed, but he continues pushing for casual sex in spite of a woman's lack of interest, he's likely to hear angry and bitter remarks from that woman, especially if she has good self-esteem and no interest in compromising it just to sexually satisfy a stranger.

Boomer women understand the connection between emotional and physical intimacy and while they were very amenable to casual sex in the 1960's and 1970's, they prefer sex in the context of a loving relationship today. They recognize that casual sex is not a path that often leads to a lasting relationship.

Sometimes Mystery is Good

In decades of on and off dating, and after hearing the same from countless other men, what I know with absolute certainty is that no good ever comes from asking a woman to share her sexual history with us. Inadequacy or jealousy are the two most likely feelings a man will likely experience if he asks a woman to describe her previous lovers and her sexual history. Worse, a man will probably waste valuable time fantasizing about her other lovers and what he needs to do in order to measure up to them. This is one of those rare situations that what you don't know won't hurt you. Most men learn the hard way at some point in their dating lives that this isn't a question that needs to be asked or answered. Suffice to know that since you're both boomers, it's improbable that either of you is the other's first lover. "Don't ask, don't tell," works in this situation better than it did for the Army.

A Common Good

The joy of being with a woman who's my peer extends beyond old photographs. Sarah's frames of reference about sexuality and relationships coincide with mine. We both decided long ago that casual sex, while the norm way back when, doesn't feel appropriate now, especially in terms of establishing a long-term partnership. What wasn't so important when we were both young and struggling to create our identities is important now; frankly, sex with strangers lost its luster for us well before the HIV scare. When we make love, it's with a depth of joy that only comes with the sweet way we feel about each other, and it's less about satisfying ourselves in the moment, and more about the depth of love we feel for each other. Sex enriches our relationship because we both treat it as a way to demonstrate our depth of love.

A Champion

Since we both rallied behind the social causes of our youth, the Anti-War movement, the Civil Rights Movement, the Women's Movement, and several political campaigns, we see the world through the same social justice lens. Sarah's passion for helping the underclass took the form of mentoring a young girl, who she's still working with a decade later. That girl is now a young woman in college. The tools Sarah has given this young woman have helped her cope with a harsh personal life situation few of us will ever face. Sarah always finds time to be available to her when she needs it. Most of Sarah's boomer girlfriends volunteer to support causes intended to improve the quality of everyone's life.

Boomer Women Volunteer

I've done a fair amount of volunteer work over the past several decades, and with few exceptions, the heads of every one of those volunteer organizations were boomer women. That's not a coincidence, but rather a reflection of boomer women's determination to play an active role in change and creating a better world. Their level of compassion for others extends well beyond the environmental, charitable, child-related, and other types of volunteer work boomer women commit to. Do boomer women have big hearts? The evidence supporting this is pretty strong, and what man wouldn't feel incredibly grateful to be in relationship with a partner who has a big, open heart?

Character Isn't Baggage

Character is developed through struggle, because that's when we're tested and forced to face our demons and overcome them. Being a single mother is a major character builder, and it has created women who have strong and durable character, which has absolutely no relation to baggage. Insisting boomer women have too much baggage is ignoring what they actually do have in abundance, namely strength of character. A strong woman shouldn't be dismissed out of hand because of her strength, unless a man feels threatened by a woman who can carry her own weight in a relationship, and in life in general. Do some men still feel they need to be in charge in a relationship in the twenty-first century? While it's difficult to fathom why a man would relish that task since it's a lot of work and pressure, it's clear from negative comments about boomer women that some men still feel a need to be in charge.

Boomer Women and Fair Play

When we disagree about an issue and we're at odds, I can always count on Sarah's sense of fair play to help us move through the crisis. Like many boomer women, Sarah put herself through graduate school while working full-time. She actually had a day job, bartended at night, and went to graduate school in between. That took grit, something boomer women have in great quantity. She never puts our relationship on the breakup table when we're struggling, and has never suggested we end our relationship when difficult challenges arise. I can't honestly say I've never threatened to walk in previous relationships that have become problematic, but I never do with Sarah. She just seems to know deep down in her bones, that the only way our relationship can work is for each of us to strive for something as close to unconditional love as possible. She's taught me a lot about friendship in a relationship as it co-exists with love, and I've tried to incorporate her example into my friendships with men. They've noticed the difference and appreciate it. While I think the world of Sarah, the truth is that there are millions of similarly capable boomer women who have a relationship skill set that younger women simply haven't yet developed.

Loving Lessons

Patience has never been my best quality. In fact I've struggled terribly with impatience about many things I find difficult to muddle through. When Sarah notices I'm becoming impatient navigating my way through the type of bullshit that seems to be the nor in situations like telephone calls to airlines, she talks with me afterward, calmly and without judgment, and makes her point about my impatience as it relates to her concerns about my health. That feels entirely different than hearing someone begin a sentence with, "Why can't you just (fill in the blank)?" Her concern for me runs deep, and while we both enjoy spending as much time together as possible, when I'm working and need time alone, she's always okay with that. Boomer women typically see beyond the obvious.

Women, who have raised children, and single mothers in particular, have learned to love unconditionally, and they bring that deep, constant sense of love into their relationships with men to the ultimate degree possible in the man/woman dynamic. Women who've raised kids have good days and bad, but their love is constant. While I'm confident younger women have these qualities, only a lifetime of experiences can develop the level boomer women possess.

My partner is a boomer I know I can depend on to hold up her end of our relationship. She never balks at doing whatever's necessary to make things work between us. Her strength is one of our relationship's greatest assets. I can't imagine being in a relationship at this stage of my life, having to carry the ball on every down. That would be exhausting, and I sometimes wonder if older guys with young girlfriends don't feel exhausted from always being in charge. I also wonder if they ever wish they had a peer partner so they wouldn't always have to carry the ball.

Your Package is in Danger

A few years ago, a woman in Los Angeles cut off her unfaithful husband's penis, a horrific, incomprehensible act. The online misogyny community lit up the Internet like a Christmas tree, warning every man in America to guard his package. This ridiculous level of hype continued for months. Of course that was only the second time this had happened in recorded history, and it hasn't happened again since, but the woman haters were on fire.

It's rare to observe this magnitude of gender diminution from a woman. They just don't seem willing to sink to that level with men, even after having been mistreated by them. There's no vitriol that women feel about men that equates to that of misogynists. My single women friends put up with a lot of nonsense from men they're dating, and boomer guys are no exception when it comes to rudeness. Still, when I ask how a date was, the worst I hear is that the guy was kind of a jerk. I've yet to hear anything resembling an "all men" statement. A man who labels women bitches, simply because they don't act subordinate, doesn't have a female counterpart. I urge men who feel such disrespect for women to look inside and try to figure out why they feel as they do. I'm no psychologist, but I'm smart enough to know that women bashers need help because women haven't earned that level of disrespect.

Women Just Know

Boomer women know that no argument gets resolved in a relationship unless or until both people can discuss the problem from an emotional place. A man who tells his partner that he doesn't think they're having enough sex isn't likely to find agreement with his thoughts, which are after all, only his opinions. The same man who is able to tell his partner that he misses the warm feeling that comes from making love is far more likely to find himself in bed with his partner.

Trick or Treat

This isn't a trick or treat situation, and it's not meant to help guys have more sex. Savvy guys are aware that they're going to be expected to hold up their end of the emotional dialogue in a relationship with a boomer woman, so they comply, not to prevail or to acquiesce, but to make themselves and their needs clearly understood. The disagreements in relationships can get resolved when both partners are able to express their feelings about why they disagree. With rare exception, every boomer woman I ever dated had the ability to resolve relationship problems on an emotional basis. I've always marveled at the ease with which boomer women are able to express their feelings.

Misguided Mire of Misogyny

I dallied with misogyny longer than I'm comfortable recollecting. I was a young man, and I wasn't confident, or comfortable in my manhood. There was a period when I treated women as if their feelings were less important than mine. I wish I hadn't and I feel badly about the women I mistreated. I hope that some men leaning towards misogyny might reconsider their attitude and try to remember from where it came. Mine was entirely about being an angry man, and feeling that women owed it to me to tolerate my anger and forgive me for it. I read anger in every misogynist comment men have written after my articles about women.

What "Balls" Really Means

I wrote an article for *The Huffington Post* in support of boomer women last year, and I was inspired to write it for many of the reasons I've already explained. Men and women wrote more than a thousand comments after that article, most, but not all in support of it. Only one from a guy, stuck in my craw. His language and tone indicated he was young and already on the wrong path. He wrote, "Ken has been emasculated by boomer women, and it's obvious he's in their pocket." My response to this misguided man/boy was short and not so sweet. "Actually, I finally grew a pair, something you might consider doing."

I'm A Better Man

Sarah is my absolute best friend, and I readily admit that she's the first woman I've ever said that about in a relationship. She has taught me by example that selflessness is not only a virtue in a partner, but a necessity. Boomer women don't seem to find the concept of selflessness difficult. I can honestly state that being in relationship with her has made me a better man. She's always willing to go the extra mile to help me when I need it. She's there for me no matter what my needs, and she never complains or makes a big deal about it. And even though I might want to return her loyalty and kindness, I don't feel confident I'm as capable as she is, all of the time. That said, I've learned to put her needs ahead of mine when it's appropriate. The more energy I put into our relationship, the more I seem to draw from it.

Chapter Two:
Boomer Men

I've aimed a fair amount of what I've written about boomer dating at boomer men. I've always been an outspoken fan of boomer women and I've dated boomer women exclusively. I met my partner, who's a boomer woman online, and I mention this because it would be disingenuous to suggest anything I didn't subscribe to when I dated.

Having said this, I'm also a huge fan of boomer men and not simply because I am one. We're a much-maligned group and, although I feel many of us might do better in terms of our dating behavior, most of us are what women like to term "good men." We're different enough from boomer women that an explanation of our differences might help women understand us better and perhaps be patient with us when we occasionally drop the ball dating them.

It's wrong-headed to paint all men with the same broad brush because we're not all alike. There are a myriad of factors about boomer men that boomer women would benefit from knowing and may be unaware. Men may be easier to figure out in the moment because we're linear thinkers but that doesn't mean we're not complex or complicated. Most boomer men are good-hearted, and while many of us admittedly struggle with dating, we're open to improving our performance. But we're not entirely sure what better looks like. That's one reason I wrote *The Boomer Guide to Finding True Love Online,* to share what better might mean for boomer men and women.

The Women's Movement came as a surprise to all men, boomers included. While our fathers went off to work every morning and brought home the bacon, our mothers stayed home and boomer men viewed boomer women in that context. Men were the breadwinners and women were their backups. Few mothers worked when I was a boy and most families survived on the father's paycheck. In most families, fathers made all of the financial decisions and, while they may have also been appreciated, women weren't held in the same regard as men.

The fly in the ointment in that paradigm was that many of our fathers were seriously flawed men, and one of their flaws was that these men failed to understand that women weren't going to be satisfied sitting on the bench while they played. This misstep was due to our lack of vision and steadfast resolve to maintain the status quo.

Most boomer boys grew up with fathers who were emotionally unconscious or minimally skilled, and very few fathers ever spoke from an emotional place other than anger. Their anger was rarely explained in terms of how they felt about what their sons did that made them feel angry. Instead, they talked about what they thought about their sons, which left boys in the dark regarding what fathers felt about them, or anything for that matter. We guessed a lot and were often wrong.

With the exception of the family dog being killed by a car, I never saw my father cry, and if there ever was a man who needed to let loose and howl at the moon, it was my broke, frustrated father. Many boomer boys were subjected to a father's ridicule if they didn't live up to his expectations, which were often so loosely defined they were difficult to divine, let alone achieve. It's no wonder few of us wanted to be like our fathers, and this attitude only hardened further when we became teenagers. The sixties defined young boomer men and put them on a path that was in direct conflict with our fathers.

Young boomer women weren't the first generation of women to become political, and, like the women who came before them who demonstrated for Suffrage, they wanted more power as women in the culture. Young boomer men rejected most everything about their fathers. A short list of rejections would include our fathers' politics and blind faith in government, sexual attitudes, tastes in music, fashion, and the now debunked notion that a job for life was worth suffering for.

Many white boomer men felt the sting that was the injustice of segregation and marched with African Americans to ensure their civil rights, and not always with their father's blessings. I still remember when I was sixteen, marching with other boomer men, black and white, for what most of white America took for granted but was still denied to many African Americans.

While boomer women demonstrated to end the war in equal numbers with men, none faced the draft, which made it less threatening for them and more ideological. When I was going off to college my father told me at dinner that it was my duty to go to war if my government said so. I shouted my response at my father, who had sat out WWII, without a lick of respect, "Fuck that, if you think the Vietnam War is so righteous, you go." His attitude about the government, right or wrong, made me wonder if he'd be prouder to have a folded flag than a living son. I was one of millions of boomer boys whose fathers held naive beliefs about their government.

I'm not sure who boomer girls' heroines were because I wasn't paying attention to that aspect of their lives, but young boomer men's heroes were different than their fathers'. The dictionary defines a hero as a person who is admired for great or brave acts or fine qualities. John Wayne was our fathers' hero but he was a false hero to young boomer men. He starred in a film about Vietnam, which we resented, especially as we faced going off to war. He'd only been a hero in films and had never fought in a real war. John Wayne was just another phony, whose patriotism wasn't backed by his actions, just like my father.

We believed in our heroes because they were authentic, and they encouraged our hopes and dreams to be unique and bolder than our fathers and make the world a better place for everyone. Bob Dylan was our poet philosopher, taking on every issue young men struggled with. The Beatles experimented with psychedelics and Eastern religion, which caused us to further rethink lives that were already in conflict with our fathers' generation. John Kennedy told us we could achieve great things if we worked hard, and Martin Luther King changed an entire nation's cultural attitudes and laws through personal sacrifice. There were many other men we looked up to and modeled after but few, if any, were from our father's generation. They represented the past and we were looking ahead.

The antiwar movement embraced the sex, drugs, and rock and roll mantra, which was a major break from our fathers' generation on all three counts. There was a new gold standard for our generation and it didn't include war. I cried out of sadness and outrage when my boyhood friends began coming home in flag draped boxes, while politicians shamelessly spouted patriotic rhetoric about appreciating their service. We refused to follow the past because we saw ourselves as a bright new future. Our differences with our fathers' generation put us in conflict with them and that became a war of sorts that was fought over dinner tables and on the streets all over America. We shouted epithets during our antiwar demonstrations that our fathers couldn't have imagined uttering. "One, two, three, four, we don't want your fucking war" was shouted at a President, and that deeply offended many of our fathers, who were passive about their government's actions. Unfortunately, none of this contributed to creating any emotional awareness in us other than anger at a President; none of our youthful rebellion and enlightenment bore any relationship to how we treated young women.

Boomer boys grew up competing with other boys in sports and, while most of us had best friends, there were major limitations to what we shared with them. Unlike young girls who frequently talked about their personal issues together, young boys didn't share their personal secrets with anyone. Like our fathers, we remained bottled up. This was due in part to the competitive nature of boyhood friends and not wanting to appear weak. The other reason was that few of our fathers ever talked to us regarding their feelings about anything and we didn't know that men could talk about their emotions and still be considered manly. We also didn't learn how.

This lack of emotional intelligence may not have served us when we were younger, but in later years it created huge dating problems. Women didn't shy from sharing their feelings with each other, and they left men in the dust in terms of developing emotional intelligence. Some of us are still trying to catch up with them while many remain oblivious to the reasons for the gender gap. This shortcoming has a long history and it isn't necessarily our fault since it was a lesson young boys weren't taught. That said, men can become more capable if we're treated with compassion and kindness instead of anger and disgust.

Boomer men still remain secretive about their personal lives in much the same way they did as boys. My home was wracked by violence and anger, but I never said one word about this to anyone during my troubled boyhood years, not even to my closest friends. In fact I never shared my pain about anything with anyone until I was in my forties. I was ashamed of the violence in my home and I didn't want to appear different than other boys. Being tight-lipped about my feelings became my model for what I thought of as manhood. I continued my stoic attitude as an adult. I was an angry, macho, tough guy into my forties before I woke up to the suffering my flawed behavior was causing me, and everyone around me. I finally faced my demons with help from other men who didn't judge me.

Some boomer men still retain old-fashioned notions of women. A boomer guy once told me that a woman's best use was as a pleasure unit and that he'd never had an intelligent conversation with a woman, including his wife. I was stunned and so were the other men who heard this declaration. Some men enjoy women but don't necessarily value them as peers. We remember that women marched with us to end a war, which spared thousands of young boys from dying, and while we were grateful for their help few of us returned the favor when women demonstrated for their rights a decade later.

In case you don't remember it that way, take a look at old photos featuring thousands of women demonstrating for women's rights. If you look for men you'll notice a few, but nowhere near the equal numbers of women who marched with young men to end a war. Our gratitude for their help was a mile wide and an inch deep, and it took a long while before it included equality.

There wasn't any consciousness about male behavior until women began labeling some of us male chauvinist pigs, which I admit made me more angry than sympathetic until I realized that, to a great extent, they were right. While I didn't feel proud of my knuckle-dragging attitude, there weren't any male leaders telling us much about how we should treat women either. Equal rights for women was a hard lesson for lots of boomer guys, and the confusion we felt in our twenties and thirties about a woman's place in society is still a conundrum for some boomer men today. Their confusion takes the form of not knowing what appropriate behavior looks like when dating boomer women.

Boomer women had Gloria Steinem and other strong women to lead them into the twenty-first century. Boomer men didn't have any male leaders to point out a new, better, workable path with women and we stumbled when women challenged our behavior. This was a difficult time for young men whose motives may have been fair-minded, but whose attitudes were not. Men that had sex with lots of women were considered cool by our culture, but women who were promiscuous were labeled sluts and whores. Double standard? Sure, and it continues today.

In the eighties and nineties, when boomer women were feeling empowered, they began demanding men become more aware of their needs. Women didn't really know what being manly meant beyond wanting men to be more "sensitive." Some guys simply took them literally and became emotional without reason, which fell flat with all men and most women. Women wanted men to be more manly, but didn't have a clue what that was supposed to look like. What became clear though was that men who let their emotions run wild without purpose or focus were not at all what women had in mind when they issued their challenge. Slobbering men didn't equate to their notion of manhood.

Some of us decided that since women couldn't explain what they meant about how men should behave, that we didn't have any obligation to move in their direction. There weren't any men in the popular culture that other men could look up to in terms of evolved male behavior and clearly just being emotional without purpose wasn't going to work for men or women. Men, who wept aiming to please women, pleased no one.

A few authors wrote books about men, Sam Keane's *Fire In The Belly,* and Robert Bly's *Iron John,* in particular; both spoke to male behavior. Their writing spurred some of us to dig deeper into our manhood to figure out what a better version might look like. No one wrote anything concerning how doing that was going to make us better men and in particular, better men in women's eyes. Bly wrote about mythological heroes and Keane told us to get together in groups to help each other understand and improve ourselves as men. Both were good starts but neither gained much traction.

I was inspired to start a men's group after a Robert Bly day twenty-five years ago, and while I found his mythology fascinating it wasn't easily applicable to my daily life. Still, he did get me out of my head and into a room with seven other men, my men's group, which turned out to be a terrifying, but rewarding experience. Sam Keane lived nearby and he was my go-to guy who I called on occasion to help me get my group on a better path. While it became confrontational, it was aimed at working on evolving into empowered men, which meant understanding that expressing our feelings comes from a place of strength, not weakness.

I've written about this journey in several articles and in a book I wrote, *Act Like a Man*, in which I chronicled eight men coming together and finding purpose and a methodology to free us from our old demons as well as new problems. Relationships with women were, and still are the main issue we discuss decades later. Getting it right with women isn't second nature to any men I've ever known. What's clear is that the men who have the most success in relationships have done some inner work with help from other men to achieve that success.

I'm not suggesting that boomer women are responsible for boomer men's behavior, but women can help, albeit by remaining responsive, not reactive. It's not a secret that most men find expressing their feelings difficult at best, and impossible at worst, but women can play a positive role to enable the kind of emotional dialogue that creates and deepens intimacy in a relationship.

A woman who wants to know her man's feelings about her or their relationship, needs to know beforehand that when a guy shares his feeling with a woman he's expressing his absolute truth. Since he's telling his truth, the appropriate response can't ever be judgment about it. A woman's feelings in reaction to a man's truth are the only appropriate response. What I know, without a scintilla of doubt, is that if a woman responds in a judgmental manner when a man attempts to express his feelings, that will be the last emotionally based conversation she will ever have with him.

An Uneven Playing Field

A man who ventures onto this uneven playing field with a woman doesn't want to compete for who's the most skilled at this conversation. He is willing to participate in this dialogue because a woman has made him feel he's going to be safe, which to a man means immune from hearing her opinions about his feelings.

Certainly a woman may share how what he shares makes her feel, but that's the extent of what's acceptable if she hopes to ever engage him in the emotional dialogue arena again.

Note of Caution to Women

I advocate for men to be emotionally honest with women, but with a disclaimer. If a woman wants a man to share his feeling about her and their relationship, and he's willing to try, it's incumbent upon a woman to honor and respect what he shares since his feelings are his absolute truth, and as such, are not open to debate, opinion, judgment, or advice.

Men who venture into the emotional dialogue arena aren't likely to repeat what felt like a death-defying act in the first place if they're attacked for being truthful. I urge women to treat men who engage in this conversation with respect and some amount of gratitude that reflects its difficult nature. The reward for this is obvious, since his willingness to engage with you emotionally will allow the relationship to move to a deeper level.

Chapter Three:
Lessons Learned

I Play Poker Once a Month

Twenty-five years ago, when I decided to start a group of men to meet regularly to discuss our issues, I remember asking a dozen men before finding eight who felt as I did about the potential benefit of talking honestly and confidentially about our lives. Most of us were in our early forties, and a few, like Frank, were older. There were men who didn't see the wisdom of meeting with other men, and whose comments summed up a deficiency I've noticed in many men's lives, camaraderie on a deeper level than sports or political banter. One reluctant guy in particular stuck out. He was a lawyer I didn't know well, but well enough to recognize that he had acquaintances, but no real friends. "I play poker once a month with a bunch of guys. We drink beer and get rowdy, and that's about as much male bonding as I can handle." I'd heard first-hand stories about this fellow's wife belittling him in front of other men on several occasions, and I noticed his kids mostly ignored him. That his marriage wasn't a friendship left this glib guy out in the cold, in terms of ever emptying his emotional baggage cart. That's a lot of stuffed emotions to carry around, and some of that pain naturally seeped into his everyday life, but went unresolved.

Lifelong Lessons

While little girls grow up sharing their stories openly, little boys are taught to keep their feelings to themselves. "Act like a man," was what most boomers were admonished when injured or sad. While little girls play together, little boys are taught to compete. With the advent of girls' sports, that's changed some and girls are competing too. I notice however, that young girls still sit together and talk endlessly about everything under the sun, so it's clear to me why they feel comfortable continuing that behavior as women. Women's groups became popular in the early 1960's, and continue today. What lessons have women's groups learned that men could benefit from? My men's group casts considerable light on this question.

In the past twenty-five years, the number one topic at nearly every one of my men's meetings is dating and/or relationships. The conversation moves around a lot, in terms of whose relationship or what stage of function or dysfunction it's in, but no other issue has a death grip on men's hearts stronger than the man/woman dynamic. Dating, marriage, divorce, and every other aspect of relationships have been topics of conversation for decades. Does that mean the guys in my group are too dumb to glean the answers? No, but what it means is that different issues continue to arise that hobble men in relationships, and that unburdening the sense of puzzlement is the simplest way to resolve those problems.

The first stumbling blocks for men to hurdle in terms of getting their "stuff" out and on the table for discussion is fear and lack of trust, the same two hurdles that have prevented men from sharing their painful problems with each other since cavemen bumped chests to celebrate a successful hunt. Fear takes many forms and encompasses many issues between men. Fear that the other guy has more money, a bigger house, a prettier wife or girlfriend, a better job, more friends, is more intelligent, is better looking, a better athlete, and last, but in no way least, has a bigger penis. With the exception of the bigger penis, women seem to face the same differences with far less anxiety, but that's because they actually talk with each other regarding how they're feeling about those fears and differences, instead of stewing a about hem.

Trust takes a back seat when men hold their emotional cards close to their chests so that no one can seem them. What I know with clarity is that when men finally do bite the bullet and find enough strength and trust in their hearts to talk about themselves, the truth comes out, and when it does, men's hearts are set free and their spirits soar higher than most can remember ever experiencing before. Nothing feels better to a man who's been holding his feelings in for a long time than finally unburdening himself and hearing other men talk about how they felt in his situation, and what they did that helped or didn't help resolve their pain. This is precisely what men's groups are meant to accomplish, sharing experiences on an emotional level. Advice is not part of the process and as a friend once opined, unsolicited advice is the lowest form of conversation. Sentences that begin with, "you should," are never uttered between authentic friends unless advice was asked for.

Besides every imaginable aspect of relationships, a partial list of the other hot topics my guys and I have dealt with includes: unemployment, financial difficulties, raising children, health, aging, friendships, trust, and the fears around so many things men harbor beyond sharing their feelings with other men. For a man to know that he never has to suffer with his pain or issues alone again is like offering him oxygen for his suffocating heart. The first thing we do each time we meet is to ask who needs time to talk. In twenty-five years there's rarely been a meeting that ended before each man who needed time received it. Someone once asked me, "Haven't you guys worked out all your issues by now?" My response was, "Doesn't anything new ever come up in your life?"

One fellow wrote a comment after an article I'd written about men's groups for *The Huffington Post* that clearly demonstrated the problem for many men. "Men who talk about their feelings with other men are wimps," he insisted. My response to him was, "A wimp is a guy who continues to inflict his issues on everyone around him rather than facing those issues with other men and resolving them."

The notion of 1960's guys drumming in the woods and using drugs is the worst myth ever perpetrated by a media whose goal too often seems to make men look foolish. Television accomplishes this well by featuring knuckle draggers on most of its sitcom programs. Sadly, too many men watch these shows, decide their fate is already sealed, and simply continue on that path.

So how does this male conundrum affect boomer men while dating and in relationships with boomer women? Too many boomer guys still believe that telling women what they're thinking about them and their relationships is just as valuable or the same as telling them what they're feeling about them. Telling a boomer woman on a first date that he can't think of a reason why she isn't interested in having sex with him, and that he thinks there's something wrong with her for not accepting his offer, exemplifies the "I think versus the I feel" dichotomy. A boomer woman, who refuses his invitation for first date sex, typically does so on an emotional level. "You know, I'm just not feeling safe or comfortable about having sex with you or any man who's a stranger for that matter. It would make me feel more sad than satisfied."

Boomer guys who are recently single, and whose only frame of reference for boomer women is the 1960's or 1970's, may not fully comprehend why they're being sexually rejected decades later by the same women who practiced free love willingly and, sometimes, even aggressively. These men are stuck in a sexual time warp, which they might consider breaking out of by allowing in some twenty-first century light.

Mike's Wake-Up Call

I'd known Mike long enough to recognize that his skepticism about boomer women was the result of his relationship with his ex-wife who was, in fact, an angry woman. While her anger had its roots in her family, and not with Mike, it stuck with him anyway. He also had a middle-aged woman tenant who was bitter about how boomer men had treated her. She commented to Mike on numerous occasions that she felt middle-aged women were disposable, which added to his growing concerns about dating them. He didn't get his wake-up call regarding boomer women for quite a while.

Mike divorced after a twenty-year marriage that left him a single father of two preteen boys. He was bitter about being designated the physical custody parent and he struggled with the challenge that role entailed. Since I'd been a single dad, Mike and I talked about single parenting frequently, and he gladly accepted any experiential advice I had to offer. After a year or so Mike had become the quintessential dad, deeply involved in his sons' lives. He worked from his home, so he was physically available for his boys most of the time, which helped him stay on top of their development into young men.

Mike began dating shortly after his wife left him with his boys, and he met Michelle, a woman twenty-five years younger, after a few months. In fact, he was looking for a day sitter for his sons, but that never happened because they became involved instead. What started as a sexual relationship turned into a live-in situation that lasted for ten years. Whenever we spoke about his relationship with Michelle, Mike would wax eloquently about every aspect of their sexuality. Since his marriage hadn't included much sex he was thrilled to have such an eager partner.

It was during their ten-year, live-in situation that his girlfriend actually became a woman. I couldn't help but notice her metamorphosis from girl to a woman, since it was even physically obvious. Near the end of their relationship she began a new career that required additional education beyond her college degree. Shortly after, she left Mike for one of her professors. Mike was devastated, angry, and bitter, and he talked about feeling used and betrayed each time we spoke. He'd helped her with her new career and hadn't an inkling she was seeing another man until she told him she was leaving. We talked daily for many months while Mike vented his anger, born from betrayal. Eventually, he was able to let it go, for the most part, but aspects of it hung on for a long time.

When he thought about dating again, he worried that a decade with a young woman had ruined his chances for a relationship with a woman his age. He still talked about the incredible sex, her tight young body, and her willingness to experiment sexually at the drop of a hat. He didn't have any hope that a boomer woman could meet that high standard of sexual behavior, especially since his ex-wife had little interest in sex.

I mentioned to Mike on several occasions, that while he'd had stellar sex with his young partner, he hadn't developed a relationship that embraced either trust or friendship. They'd ostensibly been teacher and pupil, and when the pupil became a teacher, there wasn't a friendship left to carry their relationship. Since she'd cheated on Mike, there hadn't been any trust built between them either.

Mike dated a few women, mostly boomers, but none that inspired a second date. A few months into dating, he went to a Sunday afternoon party hosted by a boomer woman whose guests were all boomers, and he met Karen, a boomer woman just a few years younger. They talked late into the evening, both thoroughly enchanted and thrilled to meet a fellow boomer who was evolved and open enough to discuss their life. They saw each other nearly every day, and their friendship grew like a weed.

Mike brought up trust since he'd been stung by the lack of it in his last relationship, they addressed it, and they agreed it had to be implicit in a relationship. They spent their time together hiking, talking, holding hands, and kissing lightly. They talked about the need to accept each other, but leave room to work out issues that could prove problematic. This level of conversation was new for Mike, since neither his marriage nor his relationship with Michelle had included much meaningful dialogue. Mike told me he felt a best friendship with Karen and that trust was already a given in their relationship. He was beyond satisfied, but there was still a hurdle left to jump. Sex remained an unknown.

When both felt ready, they moved their relationship into the sexual realm. Mike was surprised by, and appreciative of,

Michelle's sexually open attitude. She'd been a mom and was divorced for a decade, during which she'd experienced a level of sexuality she'd missed in her marriage. She felt as if she'd wasted years in a sexual desert with her husband and was anxious to move that aspect of her life along quickly. She experimented with men prior to meeting Mike and, while sex was okay, she felt certain that what was missing in those sexual experiences was a heart connection.

Since their relationship was also a best friendship, they helped each other with issues that arose not only between them, but also outside the relationship, the way best friends do. Mike hadn't ever had a best friendship with a woman with whom he was sexual before, and didn't know it was even possible.

Michelle brought her sense of heart-centered sexuality into her relationship with Mike, who was astounded by her sexual attitude and her desire to please him. Mike mentioned to me that Michelle's body wasn't as youthful as Karen's, but that the emotional component she brought into their relationship more than made up for that. It's been four years since Mike and Michelle met, and their relationship continues to grow. I've never seen Mike happier in the thirty years I've known him. When I asked him what he thought about boomer women recently, his comment was short and sweet, "Boomer women are the bomb." In Mike's world, there is no higher compliment.

Mike had been skeptical, even cynical, about boomer women before he met Michelle, and he'd bought into many of the myths about them, particularly the angry, bitter myths, some of which were left over from his marriage. He said he felt ashamed he'd ever spoken badly about boomer women, and admitted he'd mostly repeated what he'd heard other boomer men say about them, which was easy since his ex-wife had in fact been angry. Mike isn't unique in terms of holding onto old stuff about exes, boomer women or younger, and he isn't unique in terms of evolving to the point he could let that old stuff go. His happiness in a relationship depended on putting the past behind him.

A Cautionary Tale

Another man's story about a past, painful relationship with a woman took an entirely different turn. That Frank was highly educated made no difference in terms of his story, and that he'd allowed his entire adult life with women, including his wife, to be colored by one painful experience was unnecessary and sad. His story is a cautionary tale for every man who has shut down his heart after having it broken, rather than healing it and being open to love again.

Frank

When I started the men's group twenty-five years ago, there was one fellow in particular who stood out at our first meeting because of his bizarre attitude about women, boomer or otherwise. "A woman's best use in life is as a pleasure unit," he declared that first evening, and repeated at subsequent meetings. Sometimes he added, "I've never had an intelligent conversation with a woman in my life," and when asked if that also applied to his wife, he answered, "including my wife." The other seven of us couldn't imagine from where such disrespect for women sprang, but he declined to explain each time he was asked. After listening to Frank disparage womankind for several years, and boomer women in particular, one fellow felt he'd hear about all he could stand without some explanation, and he pushed Frank hard to share the truth behind his misogynistic statements.

The group had spent years developing trust in terms of the members sharing their truths with each other without recrimination. Frank had watched other men dig deep and share their painful stories, so his opening up wasn't by any means the group's first experience in that arena. In what was a rare, emotional moment, Frank dropped his head into his hands and began weeping quietly. We were stunned since we'd never seen

Frank show any emotion other than anger. We waited patiently, giving him sufficient time to recover so he could explain both his attitude and his sadness. His story explained everything about his poisoned attitude toward women and it's a story that other men may share if they feel that women are the source of their pain.

Frank's voice broke several times before he could settle down and tell his story. "I was in the Army, stationed in Seoul at the American Embassy, in Intelligence. I met a Korean woman, Kim, and we fell in love. We spent as much time together as my Army posting allowed, and after a year we began talking about marriage. We made plans to spend a long weekend together and to meet at the train station. We planned to meet on the train platform at 1:00pm. I arrived early and sat on the platform bench, holding a bouquet of flowers. After waiting for half an hour, and fearing we'd miss the train, I called her from a telephone booth. Her response was rapid and matter of fact. 'I can't talk with you or ever see you again.' That was it, and she hung up. I staggered to the bench and flopped down, stunned and sick to my stomach. The wilted flowers reflected my broken heart."

We asked Frank several obvious questions. Had he called her back or gone to her home to discover what was behind her dumping him in such a matter of fact and cold manner? "No, I didn't, and even today, I'm not sure why I didn't. I think I was too afraid of facing her and hearing her reasons in person."

Did her parents like him? "I'd only met them once or twice, and they'd been distant, but polite with me. Her father had been an officer in the Korean Army, which may have played a role, but I don't know with any certainty. I thought about pursuing the answers with Kim, but the pain from my broken heart kept getting in the way."

What had he done to ease his horrific pain? His answer explained precisely why he still suffered so terribly, thirty-five years later, but it didn't hold up with the group, because our own experiences regarding emotional pain completely debunked his response. "I stuffed that pain deep down inside that day so it would never hurt me again." When we told Frank that every one of our experiences regarding stuffing pain were the same, that it never makes the pain disappear, but actually keeps it alive and well, instead, Frank nodded in begrudging agreement.

Did he ever see or talk with her again in the following thirty-five years? Frank's answer stunned us. "My wife and I were at an airport twenty-five years after this incident, and I actually ran into Kim in an airline lounge. She was still beautiful, and my heart raced and sank just like it had decades before. She was with her husband, an American by the way, and all I could think of was, why him and not me? I didn't introduce her and she didn't introduce me. It was nearly as painful as the day she broke up with me. I looked over my shoulder as my wife and I got onto our flight, and Kim was still looking at me. Fuck! I can't believe how much it still hurts."

When someone pointed out to Frank that his entire attitude about women likely came from this train platform incident, he nodded affirmatively again. After several years of talking out our pain, most of which came from past experiences, we wondered what Frank was thinking about while we were having those conversations.

Frank's story actually got worse. He admitted that he'd married his wife on the rebound very soon after getting unceremoniously dumped. His unsuspecting wife still didn't know the reasons behind the absence of emotional intimacy in their marriage, or why Frank had cheated on her since they married. Frank's rationale for women hating didn't sit well with any of the other men. While we'd all experienced heartbreak with women, we'd worked our way through it and left it behind. There wasn't any sympathy for Frank beyond feeling his pain in the moment, because his lifelong pain was entirely preventable. Even the few years he'd wasted in our group by not copping to his story seemed like an insult, since it indicated he hadn't trusted us enough to share his story. It might have cut his pain short, even if only by a few years. Stuffing his pain became a self-imposed, life-sentence of anger, pain, and failed relationships. He'd spent his entire life without enjoying intimacy or vulnerability with any woman other than the one who had broken his heart.

I asked Frank the last question of the evening. Now that he had gotten his story out and understood the reasons behind the lack of intimacy in his marriage, did he feel it might be worth discussing with his wife? Wasn't there a possibility they might still create the intimacy their marriage had sadly lacked? His answer reflected the results of a lifetime of deceit. "No, I can't have this conversation with her. I don't trust her enough." When I asked him what he meant by that statement, he replied, "She'd hold it against me forever." In that moment, I actually did feel sorry for Frank, because when telling his partner the truth is trumped by his fear of the consequences, his relationship wasn't a refuge from pain, it was a source of it.

It's likely other men's comments about boomer women being angry and bitter come from a similar place of pain, rejection, and suffering related to breaking up with a woman. Like Frank, they allow a particularly painful experience to color their attitude about all women. But there are other types of experiences that can cause what I think of as the "Frank Effect." Relations between the sexes are still evolving since the Women's Movement of the 1960's, and it isn't clear yet to some men, especially recently divorced men who haven't been single in decades, what women want or expect from them. Their bitter, angry comments reflect their confusion, frustration, and the resulting pain.

"I Love You" Isn't Easy to Say

Men struggle with sharing their emotions with women for the reasons I mentioned, but there's another issue that keeps men's feelings buried inside them. It's difficult for a man to trust a woman with his heart, especially if he's experienced a painful breakup, whether he instigated it or not. The notion of sharing how he is feeling about a woman in a relationship actually runs deeper than just fear. It encompasses trust, and that's not a commodity most men have in abundance for anyone. As my mentor used to opine, "Where there's no trust, there's no love." He was right of course, and while trust, between men and women is essential, it needs to be created gently and consciously.

Tom

Tom is a longtime friend, and we've shared many personal stories over the past twenty years. He shared a story with me that made the case for women being sensitive about men's feelings when men share theirs. He was in a relationship with Karen, whose sense of pacing was faster than his. She wanted to talk about marriage, but Tom was reluctant to go there. When she asked him what the problem was, Tom told her his story that explained his hesitation.

"I have trust issues with women that go back to my mother, who frequently betrayed me, even after assuring me she wouldn't. I was married to a woman for a few years that repeated this pattern of betraying my trust. I want you to know that I'm working on my trust issue with women, but I haven't reached the point that I'm comfortable fully trusting women yet." Karen said she understood, and added that she appreciated his willingness to come clean about his reasons for going slow.

A few weeks later when Karen brought up marriage again, Tom reminded her that he wasn't ready to have that conversation yet. Without a moment's hesitation, Karen blurted out, "Yeah, sure, I'm paying the price for your mother and ex-wife." Tom was stunned, but he managed to explain that using what he'd shared with her on an emotional basis against him in an argument, betrayed his trust. Karen begrudgingly agreed. Then a month later the same scenario played out with the same result. Tom told Karen that he was leaving the relationship because he didn't feel safe trusting her with his feelings. Karen may or may not have been Tom's ideal partner, but without trust, there wasn't going to be any love.

A Sacred Trust

I've never experienced anything as hurtful as Tom's story, and I've heard many similar stories. The potential for a relationship to crash and burn around trust, related to sharing feelings exists. Are boomer men more trustworthy than women? Of course not, but boomer women are far more comfortable in the emotional dialogue arena, and since they're more at ease having this conversation, they need to keep in mind that this is a struggle for men and respect men for their efforts.

Men's Demons

The lack of willingness men have to talk about their feelings is in great part due to their lack of trust around sharing their feelings. There's a voice in a man's head that keeps telling him that his feelings are no one else's business, and that no one has a right or a need to know them. The voice also tells him that it's unmanly to talk about his feelings with anyone. Men may have friends for decades and never share how they're feeling with them. This is beyond old school; it's old movies from the 1950's, but many of the strong, silent types back then were miserable in real life.

Men may go through several failed marriages and still not understand that their ex-wives quit those marriages out of frustration related to their inability to talk about marital problems from an emotional place. When the dialogue is, *I think*, versus, *I feel*, the argument becomes circular, and never gets resolved.

Pogo Was Right

Pogo, a newspaper cartoon many boomers remember from our youth, once said 'He'd met the enemy, and it was us." The emotional honesty issue between men and women is based in the fear men harbor around talking about their feelings, something they just aren't confident doing. In truth, boomer men come by this disability honestly since as boys we weren't raised to talk about how we felt. In fact, the contrary was more often true. A boy who was injured was instructed to suck up his pain and act like a man. As men, we continue to suck up our pain and not talk about our feelings, and we fool ourselves into believing we're acting like men. Most conflicts with women arise when a man wants something from a woman but doesn't know how to ask for it on an emotional level. And since that's the level his wife or girlfriend is most comfortable, a man's needs may go unmet. Eventually, those unmet needs turn into conflict.

Nothing to Lose

Men have everything to gain and nothing to lose by developing the ability to share how they're feeling with women as well as with other men; their children will appreciate it too. The first idea a man needs to embrace is that no woman will attack, judge, or ridicule him for sharing how he feels. In fact, unless he's sharing his feelings with a sociopath who has no feelings for anyone beside herself, a man will be treated with respect and appreciation for opening the door to his emotions.

True Heroes

Perhaps a man imagining he's a hero in anyone's eyes simply because he bites the bullet and becomes emotionally fluent is a stretch for him, but not necessarily for the woman in his life. Sure, running into a burning building and saving people is the stuff of heroes, but heroism takes many forms. I suggest a man ask the woman he's in relationship if she considers his willingness to talk about their relationship from an emotional standpoint, heroic stuff. She just might say yes, especially if she'd like more of the same.

Few Exceptions

I've been working on my ability to have this type of dialogue with women for a while now, mostly with help from my guy friends. It's been tough slogging at times, and I resisted at first because I was certain it would make me appear less manly. In fact, when I held up my end of this dialogue with women, nearly all considered my behavior evolved, which in truth embarrassed me at first. I remember one woman in particular that I was arguing with about the emotional nature of boomer men. When she mentioned that few of the men she dated were as evolved as I appeared to be, I turned bright red.

After we spoke further she helped me understand that to her, my willingness to talk about my feelings in a relationship was evolved behavior. That didn't seem like such a high bar at the time, but in candor, my experience talking with other boomer men indicates many remain unwilling to engage with women on a feeling level.

Conflict and Resolution

My partner is a very social person, and for a while she booked every weekend for us to spend time with her friends. At first I wasn't sure how to handle this since it was over the top in my experience. I noticed I was bristling and getting pissed off, but couldn't really get my arms around the reasons why. Then I got in touch with my feelings around being annoyed, and I was able to articulate them. When I told her that I was feeling claustrophobic, and pushed to do something I didn't feel comfortable doing, she acknowledged my feelings immediately.

Sarah and I discuss each weekend as it approaches now, and she doesn't accept any invitations until we've had a chance to talk about them. She respects my feelings around excessive socializing and I respect her need to see her friends. We try to compromise to find a balance that works for both of us. Sometimes she spends time with her friends alone and, when she does, it's without any rancor between us. She heard me, and she respected my feelings because I was able to articulate them with her. Had I simply insisted I didn't think it was cool to spend so much time with her friends, she wouldn't have known why I felt that way, and might have chalked my attitude up to my being a reclusive guy. Boomer women know how to cut to the chase, in terms of resolving relationship issues, and they know it's only through sharing feelings that resolution is possible.

Chapter Four:
Emotional Honesty

Emotional honesty should be the goal from the first date, because emotional clarity is what keeps even a fledgling relationship on a healthy path. Emotional honesty is about more than simply telling the truth. It's about being able to share your feelings about yourself, the other person, and the relationship in the moment. Absent this ability and the trust that it fosters, a new relationship quickly founders, as a couple becomes mired in circular arguments pitting I think versus I feel statements that guaranty problems won't ever get resolved.

There's an immutable link between emotional honesty and emotional intelligence, and the former depends entirely on the latter. When I wrote an article about why boomer men need to be emotionally honest with boomer women, in *The Huffington Post*, the article received over 2,100 comments, an extraordinary number to weigh in on any issue. The comments were heated and equally divided between men and women. The women universally supported my premise, while the majority of the men said it was a disastrous path to follow. That split spoke volumes about the rift between boomer men and women. Nearly all of the one thousand men offered the same three reasons for eschewing emotional honesty with women. They were certain they'd be ridiculed, abused, or dumped. Their fear was palpable.

No Guts, No Glory

I felt compelled to follow up this article with another in *The Huffington Post*. I pointed out that every reason men offered for not being emotionally honest with women in relationships was fear based, and that fear is never a good place for men to come from, whether in a relationship, or any other aspect of their lives for that matter. The comments from men after this article were more open to hearing the reasons why emotional honesty is in fact a good path to follow with women. Perhaps women can take heart in this, because it does demonstrate that men are willing to listen about something as frightening as talking about their feelings.

I'm not a therapist, and the lessons I share regarding emotional honesty weren't learned in therapy either. This is real people's everyday behavior that has nothing to do with therapy and everything to do with personal experiences—mine, and those of thousands of *Huffington Post* and *AARP* readers who have shared their thoughts and feelings about emotional honesty with me.

Successful relationships—lasting relationships, in which emotional truth is prized, not ignored—embrace emotional honesty. Since no one can carry the emotional ball alone or all the time, both daters have to be willing and able to practice emotional honesty. This can be difficult for men and women who lack the ability to accurately identify their feelings as they arise.

In the rest of this chapter I'll detail how men, women, and couples can work to build an emotionally honest relationship. This is the essentials, the basic nuts and bolts of dating and relationships. For many boomers recently out of long-term relationships, this may be their best opportunity to get it right. I'd be remiss, and less than helpful, if I didn't emphasize its importance and give it the space it deserves.

Being Emotionally Honest With Ourselves

While practicing emotional honesty in the context of a relationship is critical for its success, it's equally important to be honest about whom we are. When I think of the outrageously large number of dates I went on with women, that I knew from the start had little or no partner potential, my failure to be in a successful relationship isn't much of a mystery. I was addicted to being in relationship, and I wasn't being honest about how I was feeling about myself as a man, or as a potential partner with women I knew in my heart I couldn't co-create a long-term relationship. My self-esteem played a key role in my willingness to be with any woman who wanted me. The more relationships I had the worse I felt, until I finally woke up to the reality of my dating life, which was inextricably linked to my emotional wellbeing. When I began working on the demons that were affecting my choices I developed a short list of questions to ask myself before emailing an invitation to a woman online or responding to an email. This list may seem elementary to some but my experiences and those of my readers suggest it won't be to many others. I feel most boomer daters could benefit from asking themselves these questions before becoming enmeshed in a relationship that never had legs.

1. Does this man or woman interest me on a level deeper than just the physical?

Sex and physical warmth are both critically important ingredients in a relationship, but we all should have learned from experience that if that's mostly what's present in a relationship, it will fail as soon as the newness factor wears off. I know this sounds elementary, but it's not for many boomers, particularly those recently out of long-term relationships. I felt a physical craving to hold a woman and be held, which pushed me in the wrong direction many times.

2. Will this man or woman make my world larger or smaller?

Choosing a man or woman to date that has friends and interests outside of the relationship can make your world bigger, and conversely a man or woman who's a loner and has little going on in his or her life, can shrink your world. Someone who's capable of expanding your life is special and eminently worth dating. My partner's friends welcomed me warmly because they love her, and I enjoy spending time with them, because like her, they have many interests I share. My world has expanded since we started dating, but I knew it would when we met, because she talked at length about how important her friends were, and she introduced me to all of them in short order. While I felt overwhelmed meeting so many people so quickly, I was glad I wasn't going to be her entire world, and even more importantly, that she had social skills. She felt the same about my friends.

3. How would I feel introducing this man or woman to my lifelong friends or family? Does this even matter considering those people aren't constantly involved in your life in the way a partner would be?

Yes it does matter, because how you'd feel about introducing that person speaks to how you actually feel about them as a potential partner, in terms of your emotional needs. It isn't so much that you need your friends' or family's approvals, but rather that you want to feel proud when you introduce them to your new partner. That sense of pride derives from knowing the person you're dating is someone special, and that your friends and family will realize shortly after meeting him or her that you're being treated with respect.

4. Am I just trying to replace my last partner with a new one to make myself feel better after a breakup?

This is a cardinal dating sin. You won't be doing yourself or your dates any favors by surrendering to your loneliness by using them to alleviate your pain. Do your own healing, and don't expect a stranger to fill the role of healer.

What's In It for Men?

Let me talk to my fellow boomer guys. Want to know the biggest complaint I hear from boomer women about dating boomer men? Boomer women see that when a relationship conversation turns to opening hearts and sharing feelings, a lot of boomer guys simply tune out. Why?

Chances are, no matter the reasons or excuses offered, what prevents us from talking about our feelings with women--and even with other men for that matter--is fear. In decades working with men, I've noticed that it's fear, more than any other factor that bottles up men's feelings and renders them incapable of working with women to resolve relationship issues.

To be able to hold up our end of a conversation that involves talking about how we're feeling about our partner or the relationship, on an emotional level, we first need to address our generally lagging skills. This is key if we hope to enjoy an intimate relationship that includes the ability to work through issues with our woman. Consciously or not, most of us want to be considered good relationship prospects. Based on what I've gleaned from tens of thousands of men's comments about my relationship articles, the number of men who realize that being emotionally fluent is a prerequisite for a good relationship is increasing, albeit slowly for boomer guys.

The fear so many men harbor about participating in a dialogue with their new partners, concerning the emotional aspect of the relationship, exists on several levels. First is the fear of not being capable of holding our own with a woman in this arena. Many of us fear looking foolish, inept, weak, or unmanly. And many are unable to connect the dots between their hearts, brains, and sex drives, to create successful relationships. Since most boomer women consider becoming sexual only after an emotional component has been established, boomer guys who don't understand the heart-brain-sex drive connection, are left scratching their heads about dating and developing fulfilling relationships.

Here's what I know with absolute certainty. It's fear that's unmanly not being openhearted, and the excuses men make for not sharing their feelings with women are for the most part, covers for fear. What's the bottom line? Men won't develop healthy, lasting relationships with women until they're able to express their needs on an emotional basis, and understand a woman's expressed emotional needs too. This applies to all types of needs, not just sexual. Expressing a desire to attend or not attend social events, stating positions about child rearing, asking for help coping with work, and many other problems for which a man may benefit from a woman who understands how he's feeling. This should be reason enough for men to push through their reluctance to engage with women on an emotional level. Fear is a powerful emotional reaction that holds us back from developing and enjoying our relationships with women to the fullest. We can do better with a modicum of effort, and the benefits will extend to relationships beyond those with women. They'll also apply to relationships with family members, friends, and co-workers.

Of the many articles about dating, sex, and relationships that I've written for *Huff/Post 50*, the boomer section of *The Huffington Post*, one article garnered more than 2,100 comments in just a few days. This is a rock-star number even for *The Huffington Post*, and it reflects the relevance of the issue. Half of the comments were from women, whose support was nearly universal; half were from men, who were largely skeptical and at times outright hostile, as if their very manhood was at stake.

The article was about the need for men to be emotionally honest with women in relationships. The reasons men offered for rejecting the idea of practicing emotional honesty with women might surprise some men and most women. The reasons most commonly offered--fear of being ridiculed, rejected, abused, or dumped by women-- indicate how wide the divide between boomer men and women really is. The usual band of boys whose hatred for women reflects their fear of women, made it clear they don't feel women deserve anything from men, including honesty. The original article (from April 5, 2012) is reprinted below:

What Do Women Want Anyway?

What do these women want anyway? That was the question men frequently asked when the Women's Movement began decades ago. I was a 20-something guy and like nearly every man I knew, I acknowledged that equal pay and career opportunities for women were long overdue. Many, but not all of us fully supported women in their pursuit of equality in the workplace. In truth, that was the easy part for men.

The difficulty for men was that there were no guidelines on how they should behave with "liberated" women in relationships, and men came under a lot of fire. With nothing taken for granted and nothing off the table, boomer men suffered from considerable confusion and anxiety about dating and relationships. The lack of a clear message about what women really want from men appears to still be problematic today.

As women coalesced to support each other's reproductive rights in the 70's, many began barreling through the barricades that had defined sexual behavior for centuries. Inspired by the possibility of the uninhibited, commitment-free "zipless f*ck," as described in Erica Jong's 1973 bestseller, Fear of Flying, they stepped boldly into the formerly all-male arena of sport, or casual sex.

And lots of guys weren't very happy about women enjoying gratuitous sex. Sport sex was a man's domain, wasn't it? While it was cool -- or at least perfectly acceptable -- for guys to have as much casual sex as they wanted, women who behaved similarly were labeled sluts and whores. And it appears that times haven't changed much, because recently, a radio shock-jock labeled a young woman law student who spoke up about health insurance and reproductive rights not only a slut and a whore, but also a "feminazi." His credibility is questionable, however, because this guy is a confessed drug addict on his fourth marriage. His popularity is limited to his mostly middle-aged, disenfranchised male listeners -- and his misogynistic outburst caused more problems for him than it did for women.

Despite the misogynistic views of this particular prehistoric throwback and his exclusively male supporters, the balance has already tipped in favor of women's equality, and women are competing on an equal basis with men -- and succeeding -- in politics, education, the professions, and business. And the scale isn't tipping back. But that still leaves relationship issues between men and women unresolved. How does the success of women translate into dating and relationships?

Relations between the sexes are changing, and it still isn't clear to many guys what women really want or expect from them. Some embittered men's comments on my dating articles reflect their confusion and frustration. They express their outrage that women won't commit to them, or that women dump them for guys who are better looking or wealthier -- in short, that women are treating men the same way men treated women for as long as I can remember. Some guys feel that the empowerment of women must mean their demise. Strong women equal weak men, right? Wrong.

My sense is that what women want most from men in dating and relationships today is emotional honesty: women want to know where they stand with their dates and partners on a feeling level. In more than 30 years of working with men, I've learned that men absolutely are capable of being emotionally open and honest, but that getting to that place requires a focused effort. Saying "I like you. I'll call you soon," after a first date is easy. But if that isn't really a guy's intention, it's emotional dishonesty.

Too many guys are still uncomfortable venturing into the emotional arena. They needn't be. Emotional honesty is actually a very manly characteristic, and one sure to open doors with women. It's quickly developed, particularly with help from other men. Relating to other men on a feeling level also deepens the bond of friendship. This is a win-win in every arena.

If you don't feel comfortable opening up and sharing your emotions with the woman in your life, consider starting out by getting together with other guys who're in the same boat. Create a safe, trusting atmosphere where you can explore a better way of being a man and partner to an empowered woman. Acting like a man includes being emotionally open and honest. There's great personal strength in that.

Men who insist that women's rights have hurt them in relationships reflect their unwillingness to look deeper into their own behavior. There's a strong and inexplicable desire to maintain the status quo, even though it's a losing position. Warring with women is foolish. Remaining stuck in an anachronistic dating or relationship paradigm isolates men. Some join men's rights groups to counter women's rights, an ineffective reaction to empowered women. They might consider what kind of woman wants to be in a relationship with an angry, frustrated man who's stuck in the 20th century.

(http://www.huffingtonpost.com/ken-solin/what-do-women-want-_b_1400390.html)

A sampling from the comments regarding the emotional honesty article is presented below. Most are from men; since the women's comments were universally in favor of my premise, I added only a few for balance.

- *If you are emotionally open and honest with a woman and don't land in the friend zone within two minutes, call the folks at Guinness World Records. I'd like to know the basis for the premise that women consider such openness manly. Ask a hundred men if they have been called "nice" by a woman, then ask how many of those women ever went on a date with them. The words "kind" and "sensitive" also spell romantic doom.*

- *I never knew how much American men hate women until I started reading men's comments on HP. It's been educational, to say the least. American women looking for a mate would do well going outside of their country's borders, to more civilized nations (across the Atlantic, specifically), where misogyny is not men's favorite pastime.*

- *You are dead wrong that what women want is "emotional honesty" from a man. But good for you because I do think what women think they want is a "sensitive" man who writes and says that what women want is emotional honesty. Then they really pine after the strutting, emotionally distant, lying cheating millionaires of the world.*

- *This article is essentially asking men to act like women, by discussing feelings with their "boyfriends" like women do with their girlfriends. What next? Will men be asked to go shopping with their "boyfriends" for shoes and jewelry, and have their hair styled and colored? Talking about your feelings to your partner is necessary, but I think that is a skill developed from having good relationships with one's mother/sisters/aunts, not by sharing feelings with other men.*

- *You hit the jackpot with this one Ken. You really hit a nerve. Who knew emotional honesty could create such a firestorm? It's so, so...ummmm, emotional! You're a good man Charlie Brown/Ken.*

- *Guys with average or above average looks who are good people are screwed these days. They better make themselves rich and beautiful if they want a chance at a relationship now. Anything less gets a rejection. I experience so much rejection because I'm not rich, I'm not a pediatrician, and I'm not George Clooney or Brad Pitt. I'm a good guy with decent looks and modest income, but what I need to do to get a chance these days in a country of super-fussy women is a lot. If it were based on personality I believe I wouldn't experience much rejection, but that is not women's main concern when evaluating a guy.*

- *The doublespeak from women is really obnoxious. They say they want a nice guy and go date jerks who abuse them. Kind of a fatal flaw, only being attracted to people who hurt them and can never be emotionally fulfilling for them.*

- *Actually, today's men have been stripped of their true nature or at least been brainwashed away from it. They don't want to be in charge, know how to be in charge, or even understand that they are supposed to be in charge. Let me say it this way . . . a million years of evolution can't be wrong and meant to be replaced by what 50 years of a runaway Liberal Agenda has brought about.*

- *It seems many men fail to understand that a relationship between empathetic people who share honest communication creates a positive sexual environment. It is difficult for most women to feel sexually aroused by an emotionally and psychologically dishonest and distant male.*

- *Emotional openness (in other words, being a feminized man) is a very manly trait? No, it's not. There's nothing manly about acting like a woman. Being able to carry on despite overwhelming emotional distress, as though nothing is wrong, while being able to complete one's work in excellent shape, maintain a healthy relationship with one's acquaintances and rivals, and be at top physical performance – that's a manly trait. Emotional openness is a sign of weakness; it invites attack, like a poorly hidden wound.*

- *Women hate feminized men anyway. Usually they are Mr. Nice Guy. They are quickly dumped into the "just friend" pile. Women simply despise these men. Treat them like rental cars. Also, being emotionally honest more often than not will end in pure grief and misery for most men. Why? Because, this is NOT what women want from men.*

- *Emotional honesty? Such a vague and loaded term, but the truth is that a man is NOT allowed to be emotionally honest with the woman in his life. Women can barely handle their own insecurities much less a man's insecurities. If a man tries opening up and showing vulnerability in a relationship, women instinctively feel he is weak (e.g. beta male) and soon end the relationship. So when you ladies ask, "Why doesn't he ever open up to me?" there's your answer.*

- *Emotional honesty? That is only for women to use as a weapon against men. Men cannot openly express their emotions, because women will declare any male emotional expression they disagree with to be false. I have never had a women explain to me how my feelings are lies and without basis in fact. I sincerely believe that I never will. Until then, I will say what I think she wants to hear --assuming I like her-- or will say nothing at all.*

- *The comments on here are awful. I can't believe how hateful American men are against women. How tragic. What a sad, sad, nation. But guys, if you hate women DON'T BREED WITH THEM. Why bother with a "relationship" with someone you hate? Just go hire a prostitute off one of them there websites. There. Easy. Done. Problem solved in one generation.*

If you want to read more of the 2,100 comments, you can find them by going to:

http://www.huffingtonpost.com/ken-solin/what-do-women-want-_b_1400390.html.

For a list of nearly 100 other articles that may also be of interest, just go to *The Huffington Post* online and type "Ken Solin" in the box at the top of the home page.

Okay, guys, I hear you, and while I'm sympathetic to what so many of you feel is the penalty for being emotionally honest with women, I disagree completely that women don't want emotionally honest men, or that there's a penalty for being emotionally honest with a woman. I've dated through portions of several decades, and I've yet to meet a woman who rejected me for being emotionally honest. But women have in fact rejected me because I was unwilling to be emotionally honest.

If you still feel boomer women prefer tough guys and guys who treat them badly, you're out of touch with what women want. The notion that a woman would hold or use a man's emotional honesty against him is a flawed at best, and while it does occur, it doesn't happen frequently. There will always be a number of men and women who have so little self-respect, that they would attack or emotionally abuse someone for exhibiting emotional honesty. But who would choose that person as a partner?

When I first read the comments I had to bear in mind that they're submitted anonymously, and on that basis people feel safe to freely reveal their fears and concerns—and their vitriol. But take a second look at the comments and the distress and fear behind them becomes more evident.

Fear Keeps Us Stuck

As I see it, men's concerns in this area stem from some common issues—most (if not all) of which connect directly to fear in some manner. There's fear of not having enough money or status, fear that they can't overcome issues from a flawed childhood, fear that they can't learn a new behavior, fear that they can't live up to a woman's expectations (emotionally, financially, sexually). Instead of directly addressing those concerns, some men insist that exploring emotions is wimpy, not manly, and not worth their time. The reality is that honesty--particularly emotional honesty-- requires strength and courage. Rather than risk it, many men dodge it by hiding behind bluster or old habits.

Hey guys, if we want to get off of the dating merry-go-round and be in successful relationships, we're going to have to carry our share of the dating and relationship load, which means meeting women halfway, and being prepared to respond to emotional dialogue in kind. Sure this is new territory for some of us, and it may take practice, but we've had to learn most everything about how we function in our daily lives. Expressing yourself may feel clumsy and confusing until you become more skilled, but learning any new skill requires practice. We need to be residents in our relationships, not guests, and we need to shoulder our share of responsibility for maintaining these relationships in a mutually beneficial way.

In the previous chapter I detailed how men might more easily practice emotional dialogue with each other. Unless you give credence to some of the negative comments above, this is a very brave thing for men to do. The fact that men grow closer with each other by deepening their friendships is another huge benefit that shouldn't be minimized. Every relationship is influenced by a man's ability to understand its emotional component, whether with a woman, his men friends, his children, or even his co-workers.

For men who fear their emotional honesty will be badly received by a woman, I want to reassure you that would be a rare occurrence. For the women reading this, I urge you to keep in mind that emotions and emotional honesty are groundbreaking stuff for lots of guys, and their efforts deserve respect and all the patience you can muster. If a man ventures into the emotional playing field, he's expressing his absolute truth and he deserves respect for that effort, not opinion or judgment regarding what he shared. Anything less will mean that the first conversation about emotional honesty, will be the last.

Truth Is Strong, Not Wimpy

When a man tells me that men who talk about their feelings are wimps, I try to help him see that it takes strength to work through old issues, and that by doing so with other men, everyone benefits. In contrast, not working on those issues, but continuing to inflict them on others (including those closest to him) is not just cowardly and cruel, but destroys all chances of developing a better relationship. Absent this change in men's behavior, men suffer needlessly.

There are many issues that men can help each other overcome within the safe, confidential confines of a small group. Divorce, unemployment, death, and fears that include the risk involved in being emotionally honest, lack of fiscal resources, and raising children. Career changes, retirement, and health concerns can be addressed without anyone expressing judgment or opinions. The confidence that a man feels knowing he has a rock-solid, steady group of caring men behind him, whose only interest is helping him move beyond his issues, is immeasurable.

It takes courage for men to sit down with other men and share their feelings openly and honestly. Breaking the inertia and fear that hold us back is the first step. Men who do this work together would never consider themselves wimps. Quite the contrary, my group began considering each other as brothers after several months because we were already helping each other work through our stickiest problems. While it takes time for a new group to gel, it doesn't take years to fully appreciate how difficult it is for men to move beyond long-standing issues.

Honesty Is Key

Even with the work we've done on developing our emotional skills, there are times when we make mistakes—individually, and as a group. Paul had been in our group for a few years. When he first married, his wife's children from an earlier marriage were toddlers, so the need for guidelines and discipline hadn't come up yet, and Paul and his wife hadn't discussed child rearing. She'd been very clear that she and the children's biological father were to act as the primary parents. Paul respected his wife's wishes and was open to this arrangement. Soon after Paul's marriage, the children's father decided that he wasn't interested in day-to-day child-rearing decisions—and the fact that Paul and his wife hadn't agreed on practices became a troublesome issue. Although Paul had no first-hand child-rearing experience, he did have common sense and a logical mind. He became frustrated since he felt he had some good lessons to share with the children. To his great surprise, Paul's ten-year marriage ended, not because of the children, but because of his wife's infidelity— he was shocked, devastated, and heartbroken.

He decided to take some time to reflect. Since it was winter in California, and Paul was an avid scuba diver, he went diving in Cozumel, Mexico to repair his broken heart. Before he left for his planned two-month stay, Paul mentioned to the group that he just wanted to be alone, go diving twice a day, and work through the issues responsible for his failed marriage. He mentioned several times, his need to be alone with his thoughts and feelings, in order to heal. The group was unanimous in supporting Paul's diving retreat because each man appreciated how important self-reflection and solitude were towards healing wounds and beginning to build a new life.

Paul came to our meeting on his return two months later, already deeply in love with Beverly, a woman he'd met in the first week of his diving retreat. Most of the guys understood that he'd rebounded, and that rebound relationships rarely work, but we also knew from experience that it's impossible and foolish to try to convince another man that his love isn't authentic, and that doing so is a prickly road to travel in the best of circumstances. We listened to Paul's story about falling in love, and instead of asking him the right questions, we backed off and congratulated him. Since not one man who listened to Paul's fairy tale believed he was behaving appropriately for a man who had just had his heart broken two months before, we should have expressed our doubts and concerns. But nothing is perfect, including our group, and as Paul waxed eloquently about discovering the love of his life on a beach in Mexico, the group chose to join in his joy rather than stick a pin in his balloon. In retrospect, our response and behavior weren't fair to Paul. He deserved better from us, and we fell down in terms of our responsibility to him.

When Paul, who was then in his early fifties, told us a month later that he was getting married, and that his fiancée who was considerably younger wanted to have children, we all woke up from his dream and began asking him the questions we should have when he first returned from Mexico.

But it was too late. Paul was so head over heels in love that he wasn't able to hear or talk about his relationship in any terms other than how terrific it felt. His feelings for his soon-to-be wife were so strong there wasn't any room for discussion. They married quickly and had a child in short order. It was Paul's dream to raise his own children, and he was thrilled to have that opportunity with a new daughter.

A few months after his daughter's first birthday, Paul began sharing some of the problems in his marriage, not the least of which was his wife's apparent lack of interest in hearing about how he was feeling about their conflicts as they arose. Her position was simple: "get over your feelings because I'm not interested in talking about them." It was clear that Paul hadn't ever talked about problem resolution when he was dating Beverly, which seemed ironic since Paul had always talked readily and easily about his feelings in the group. We knew from what Paul had shared when he first returned from his diving trip, that he was enjoying amazingly good sex, and we also knew that great sex frequently blinds a man to what else is in front of his nose.

Paul had singled me out on several occasions in the past, pushing me to talk about my feelings about women with whom I was in relationship. He hadn't been shy about this, and I shouldn't have been shy with him either. Sometimes it's a fine line to walk between being completely honest and wanting to support a man's dreams. I failed him, and as a group we screwed up by not pushing him to acknowledge critical issues he'd ignored. It seemed like he'd missed the mark by a mile and married a woman who wasn't remotely interested in emotional honesty. He'd disregarded a critical aspect of his wife's personality—and we hadn't pushed him to discuss this early on. To his dismay, Paul discovered—too late—that women don't have a lock on emotional honesty.

Had the group performed its task better, had we been able to put Paul in touch with this problem before it became insurmountable, he may have been able to incorporate emotional dialogue into his marriage's problem resolution skills. We learned a big lesson about our process: we needed to be more willing to challenge each other about important issues, like getting married hastily or divorced hastily for that matter. We count on each other now to tell each other our unvarnished truths, and since the greatest personal growth spurts seem to come when men are challenged to explain their behavior based on their emotions, we stick with our methodology, and don't obsess about the possible consequences.

The group gleaned other lessons through Paul's misfortune and the group's response. We learned (and sometimes relearned) that before committing to a long-term relationship men need to allow enough time for the heat of passion to quiet down sufficient for the reality to become clear. The struggle between their rational brains and their libidos is ongoing for men. Too frequently the libido wins out, no matter what's going on in a man's head and heart. All too often men wind up in the wrong relationships as a result. There are no magical, instantaneous solutions to overcome this rift, but talking about a relationship in a clearheaded, honest way helps. I admit that it wasn't until my early sixties that I finally figured this out. Of course, it may not be coincidence that by then my libido had diminished enough for my rational brain to listen.

Another lesson we learned, and have used consistently since our experience with Paul, is to confront each other no matter the consequences. Some of us had to overcome our fear of other men's potential anger. While that concern still exists to some degree, it no longer prevents us from doing the real work of challenging each other to explain our behavior based on our feelings. Can men help each other avoid potential land mines? Yes, of course they can. Will men always rise to this standard? That's the work that a group needs to commit to in order to be useful to its members. The process itself isn't always easy or pretty, but it does work.

Anger Management

Anger is at the top of many men's lists of issues to deal with, and while most men don't have any place to take their anger to talk about it, the guys in my group have a safe place to air their issues, including anger. Since anger is particularly devastating to a man's wife, girlfriend, children, and co-workers, it seems especially sad that it frequently goes unexamined.

I learned this from many long and painful experiences. Prior to the work I did with my men's group, I raged and carried on with everyone—and with women in particular. Eventually, I noticed that other men avoided me beyond casual conversation, and I didn't have even one solid male friendship. I was a tough guy who believed that all men had to be tough guys if they hoped to survive in our culture. Sometimes my anger came out as impatience, and sometimes as pure anger. I wanted to change my pattern. In time, by working with my guys, I finally got my anger and trust issues out in the open, and, ultimately under more control. It was with these men that I learned how important it is to be able to talk about my feelings, good and bad.

Over the years, I've watched other tough guys in my group struggle with their anger, and the men who faced their anger with help from the other men became more capable of relating to everyone on a civil basis. I realize that some men have difficulty accepting the premise that talking about their feelings is in fact manly. Once a man overcomes this fear and becomes willing to take a leap of faith and trust other men, he'll find that he's better able to get his anger under control.

While anger can be a useful, acceptable emotion if it's controlled, it's never appropriate to inflict it on anyone without purpose or explanation, and in a manner that can be heard, and has the potential to resolve conflict. Jumping up and snarling, "You really piss me off, you know that?" isn't the same as pausing, gathering your thoughts and feelings and calmly stating, "I feel disrespected when you second-guess my child rearing decisions in front of the kids, and it makes me feel angry." The former shows anger, but doesn't exhibit emotional control or rationale for anger, and it effectively closes the door to conversation and positive action. The latter explains the reason for the anger. The former elicits a reaction, while the latter invites a response, which can lead to problem resolution.

Controlling anger is critical in every venue. When I was a young salesman, a sales manager verbally attacked me at a business meeting. He had sent out a memo to each salesperson that he wanted to discuss at this meeting. I never received the memo, and the woman who worked with me never saw it either. When the sales manager asked me about the memo while I was in his office, I said I didn't know what he was referring to. He jumped up and stood over me, glowering, enraged, fists in my face, and began a screaming tirade that ended with his accusing me of being a liar. He went on for quite a while, and I was devastated. I found it so reminiscent of my father that I was powerless to move or speak.

After he finally stopped raging, he spoke with my assistant, who also said she didn't know anything about a memo. He came over to me later in the day and apologized. I was so pissed off and hurt that I couldn't even look him in the eye. I found a new job and quit the next day, but I never forgot what it felt like to be the victim of a business associate with an out of control temper. No one deserves to work with a lunatic and if you see yourself or your boss as being remotely this guy, do your work to overcome it, or suggest politely that your boss consider doing the same.

I missed the bigger picture and continued blowing up in relationships, especially with women. As bad as I'd felt being unfairly attacked, I just couldn't make the leap from that to my own behavior until I began talking about it in my group. I 'd briefly dated a woman who frequently trampled my boundaries. I didn't say anything to her, in part because our relationship was new, but mostly because (as I realized with help from the group) I often hadn't understood the reasons for my anger. I failed to focus on what I was feeling in the moment, and instead of working toward a solution, I exploded when my anger built up. Some habits are tough to break, and anger was an incredibly difficult one for me.

In time, I learned to anticipate blowing up by using Somatic Experiencing, through which I learned to recognize the feeling in my body that preceded blowing up, and then sit with that feeling instead of giving it oxygen. The feeling that a noisy train was barreling through my body always preceded my anger. Once I could quickly identify that feeling of anxiety, resentment didn't build up and my anger subsided. Somatic Experiencing, developed by Peter Levine, is a worthwhile technique to consider if your issue is anger. I learned about it from another fellow in my group who had used it successfully to get his anger under control. I also learned that the process of getting in touch with my emotions is ongoing—and critical.

The Importance of Sharing Emotions

There are numerous scenarios in which an emotion that goes unaddressed hurts the person feeling that emotion, and not those around him. Joy is a feeling that begs to be shared. A person who closes a business deal, a writer who sells a book, a person who recovers from a disease—each person needs to share that joy with someone. It's only natural for a joyful person to want to talk about their good fortune.

While good news always feels terrific, it feels far more significant if it can be shared with other people. There's a sadness associated with not having someone to share your joy with. Keeping your good news inside can feel terribly lonely after a while. Joy feels best when it's shared, and the feeling is more powerful when it is. It's terrific if your family is interested in your good news. If that's not the case, and if you don't have close friends who care about you and want to hear your story, joy may begin to lose some depth.

When a man in my group has received some good news, no matter what it's about, the rest of the group eagerly celebrates with him. Seeing the look in men's eyes when they have the opportunity to share their joy with other men is moving.

On the other end of the spectrum is grief. Just as joy is better when shared, recovery from grief is potentially faster and certainly less painful when you're not alone. Men who are facing grief—whether an impending divorce, the death of a loved one, a child's serious illness, or a myriad of other crises—can benefit greatly by sharing their grief. It's the feeling that a man isn't alone in the world with his pain that makes the difference. A man who feels the camaraderie and support from other men senses he's cared about, and in that moment his pain subsides.

Going it alone in life is entirely unnecessary, and men who are living a lone wolf lifestyle might want to consider the steps they can take to change that..

Every man experiences fear while dating, in a relationship, or some other aspect of his life, but not every man lives in fear. It's a choice. Men can face their fear, work through it, and then move on with their lives, or they can continue to allow fear to dominate their lives. If it's fear that's keeping you from sharing your feelings with women, it's worth working on to get through it. Your own happiness is at stake.

Learning to speak from the heart can feel at least as difficult and awkward as learning to speak a new language as an adult. Why is that? Mostly because speaking from the heart *is* a new language for many of us. Although immersion is generally considered the quickest way to learn a new language, speaking from his heart doesn't necessarily work instantly just because a man immerses himself in it. His emotional vocabulary will develop over time.

While fear is a powerful emotion that prevents us from developing and enjoying our relationships with women to the fullest, we can improve our skills to overcome it with a modicum of effort.

I don't think women expect men to be entirely masterful when talking about how we're feeling, but rather that we exhibit some willingness to explain our behavior based on our emotions. I assure you it's worth the effort. A decade of communicating with women through my books, articles, and website has shown me that women truly appreciate men who are willing to be emotionally open and share their feelings with them.

A Note of Caution to Women

Boomer women: Your man is probably going to need some forgiving space around how he expresses himself, particularly at first. He may well fear expressing his true feelings, because he's out of practice, his feelings have been questioned in other relationships, or he was attacked when he told his truth. It does take a leap of faith for a man to give a woman the opportunity to hear his feelings without holding back, particularly after having negative past experiences.

I want to remind women that they play a critical role in this emotional exchange. Acknowledging what a man shares from his heart, without offering opinions or judgments, will encourage more openhearted exchanges. A woman may not like what a man has to say about how he feels, particularly about her, but his truth is sacrosanct, and it's imperative that it be honored and respected. Few men will enter this emotional sharing arena a second time, with a woman who trashed his feelings the first time, because she didn't like what he shared. (Of course, the same cautions apply to men as women express their feelings.)

If you cut your guy a little slack around how he expresses his emotions instead of chastising or correcting him for not doing it as often or as well as you'd like, he'll respond more willingly the next time. We have to overcome our fear of appearing foolish with you in order to share our deepest feelings, and your encouragement goes a long way toward making that possible. If you want to hear what a man feels, you have to be willing to accept what he shares without using it against him the next time the two of you have a disagreement. Using what a man has shared about his feelings against him in an argument is a serious betrayal of trust, and as my mentor used to opine, "Where there's no trust, there's no love."

In the end, the single most important contribution a woman can make to help a man develop this skill, and feel okay using it, is just to listen without judgment. Having an emotionally honest dialogue isn't a contest. If it were, you'd likely win it--but winning might also mean losing. Practicing emotional honesty is a win-win situation, and must be viewed that way in order for it to work in a relationship.

What's In It for Women?

As I've said, women consistently appreciate men who are willing to be emotionally open and share their feelings with them. And since for boomers, the numbers are skewed against women in online dating, a man who understands and practices emotional honesty stands out for reasons other than his numerical advantage. In time, and with effort, more boomer men will get there. The fact is we all want to be loved, and we all want to know where we stand in a relationship. That's normal and it needn't result in conflict.

Learning Pacing

It's unusual when both partners feel the same depth of love at the same time, particularly in the beginning of a relationship. The notion of being in the same place or not is called pacing, and while it's ideal when both partners have the same sense of pacing, it's atypical in the dating world. Google the term "pacing" and the result is pages of links to sources who discuss the differences in speeds between men and women while developing an emotional connection.

Understanding that you may be feeling a deeper love and are more ready to take the relationship to the next level, doesn't mean that your guy will automatically follow your lead. This is when having an emotionally honest dialogue can make the difference between breaking up and staying together and working things out so the relationship can move forward. Accepting a man's pacing, which may be faster or slower than yours, is as critical as his acceptance of yours. Pacing should be discussed until both partners feel comfortable with each other's level of emotional intensity.

A plethora of comments in response to my articles indicate that some people (men, most often) have difficulty understanding that their pacing may not match the other person's, and may in fact be shocking to that person.

No matter a man's or woman's feelings about the person they're corresponding with, the fact that both are strangers and some people have more defined boundaries around sharing personal information with someone they hardly know is a critical factor to remember. Patience is key, especially in a fledgling relationship, which I define as at least a few dates, and not just back and forth emails and phone calls.

What types of questions fall into the category daters may feel belongs in the weird category? For some, just giving their full name can trigger online dating paranoia, and for others it may be the old standbys, politics and religion. Still others may hesitate to talk about where they work and what they do.

There's a comfort level that's fairly transparent once telephone conversations begin, but that comfort level isn't universal. What helps allay the other person's fear is not to make that person feel you're in a rush to fall in love, but rather that you're willing to be patient enough to allow the other person to unfold their life at their own speed.

What Is Love, Anyway?

Ingrid is a single, long-time friend with whom I enjoy talking about dating, because she has a thoughtful and well-developed perspective. She recently told me that she's shocked by how many men have told her they love her at the very beginning of a dating relationship, a few even over coffee on their first date. She's developed two rationales for this premature pronouncement. Either the guy is desperate for sex, and hopes that telling her he loves her will make that possible, or he just doesn't know how to separate authentic feelings from fantasies. Telling a first date you're in love is not exhibiting emotional honesty. Falling in love with a total stranger isn't about love, but is a delusion that frequently stems from feeling desperate not to remain alone. Not knowing the difference between authentic feelings and fantasy is a major disconnect between the head and heart. If some of Ingrid's dates professed their love because they thought that's what she wanted to hear, they were wrong on two counts: it wasn't what she wanted to hear, and it wasn't their emotional truth. In either case, Ingrid now remains skeptical about men declaring their love.

She became a skeptic after taking a few rocket rides with men who had declared their undying love and devotion, only to have those rockets crash and burn a few weeks or months later. The rocket ride relationship typically plays out with a couple falling deeply in lust at first sight, and continuing down that path without considering that there's something beneath the lust that needs attention. Rocket rides ignore everything but the obvious: someone who's as hot for you sexually as you are for them. Rocket rides nearly always end in disaster, and when they do, both people get a large dose of reality. They may be surprise because they felt so in love with each other. Still, I admit I rode lots of rockets before the pain from crashing finally woke me up.

What Ingrid has discovered works best for her, is to ask a man who just expressed his love prematurely to talk about what that actually means to him, from an emotional perspective. She's honest about being skeptical, but open to hearing him explain his lofty feelings. When she's given guys an opportunity to talk about their declarations of love, she's noticed that their answers are consistently vague. "You know, it's just a feeling I have about us," isn't very reassuring. And neither is, "Don't you believe in love at first sight?" Ingrid discovered that love at first sight is shorthand for, "Don't you want to have sex with me?"

There's no emotionally honest or supportable basis for a man to tell a woman he's in love with her when he doesn't even know her, and vice versa. Most of these situations defy an emotionally honest dialogue, because there aren't any authentic emotions to talk about, except perhaps the fear of being alone. Lust and sexual desire may be feelings, but they're not feelings that have anything to do with building emotional intimacy between a man and a woman who don't even know one another. And since—at least according to thousands of online responses-- trust is at the top of everyone's list of critical relationship qualities in a partner, telling a near stranger that you love them isn't going to instill trust.

Ingrid has learned to slow it down and not to go off to the love races. She's lost patience with men who are incapable of accessing and talking about their authentic feelings. As a result, she told the last guy who insisted he loved her at the end of their coffee date, "No, you don't." Then she told him how insulting it felt to hear a virtual stranger proclaim his love, because she knows that love is impossible in thirty minutes. She also said that she felt like she was being manipulated into believing the unbelievable, to satisfy his need to feel the high associated with falling in love. While I certainly appreciate her steadfastness not to take any more rocket rides, she's become somewhat jaded by her experiences with men incapable of knowing and sharing their real feelings. Ingrid believes that the responsibility for ensuring that a relationship doesn't go down this road is a shared one. Since she's tired of carrying this responsibility solo, she's still looking to date a man who is emotionally honest and able to express his true feelings.

Having had this conversation with Ingrid, I felt ashamed when I remember that I had told a few women I loved them early in our relationships. I realize now that what I was expressing was my excitement about meeting someone I felt had great potential, and for whom I also felt sexual heat. I've been on the other side of this dysfunctional behavior too, and I know how inappropriate it feels when a virtual stranger expressed her love for me. Frankly, I would consider it disrespectful now if a woman I hardly knew told me she loved me. It would scare me off for sure, because I'd know she either wasn't capable of knowing her own true feelings or had a very different definition of love. Being capable of discerning the differences between love, lust, and interest is a critical dating skill.

Love and Lust

To recognize love and be able to distinguish it from lust requires the ability to look into your heart for the truth. There's a world of difference between lust and love, although both are present in the best relationships. Many boomers couldn't distinguish the difference when they were younger, because hormones dictated their behavior. But we're older now, and hopefully smarter. Knowing the difference between lust and love depends on the ability to discern the difference on an emotionally honest basis. Questioning your feelings about someone you're excited about is made clearer by creating a checklist at the top of which are authentic feelings. And somewhere down the list is sexual lust. In truth this isn't difficult for most boomers, but even knowing the truth doesn't always dissuade us from going down the wrong road. Lots of issues can put us on the wrong path, and low self-esteem is one of them.

Deepening Relationships

The premature professions of love and the ensuing rocket rides that Ingrid and many other people experience, only become problematic if one or both people aren't in touch with how they're actually feeling. Some boomers may simply be feeling sexually frustrated or lonely. The word *love* is so over-used and abused, that it no longer carries the weight it deserves when uttered to a loved one. I caution boomers not to get aboard any more rockets. Boomers simply don't have time to waste chasing their own, or someone else's sexual fantasies.

As Ingrid has learned, it takes a concerted effort to practice emotional honesty and to elicit it from others. And while women are typically more in touch with their feelings, that doesn't mean that women express their feelings openly and honestly every time. Getting a sense of whether a developing relationship is a safe place to express one's deepest feelings takes time.

Emotional honesty isn't second nature to everyone, but everyone can learn to make it an integral aspect of dating behavior. In the long run, the benefits far outweigh any potential downside, which would likely just be momentary discomfort.

What's In It for All of Us?

Emotional honesty requires effort and energy., but most of all, it needs to be practiced to become comfortable around sharing it. Admittedly, many women have been using this skill for decades, but for some men (many of whom are developing this skill later in life), the practice begins with small steps.

Lots of men seem fearful about talking with women about feelings related to problems they're having individually, or as a couple. At my men's group one evening, Peter was still fuming about how angry he was with his wife because of an argument a few days before. "Every time I make a mistake she adds that to her laundry list of past transgressions. Nothing ever comes off of that list, so after twenty years together, the list is ten miles long. But the worst part is that every time we argue, she recites the entire list from memory. Can you imagine how frustrating that is?"

Peter's admission seems to contradict the gender lore that men can have an argument or fight, and then quickly move on without stewing, or having it affect their day (as is thought to be typical of women). The apparent ease with which many men move on to other topics can leave women feeling that either the issue doesn't matter to the man, or that he's trivialized its importance and moved on. Since I've known a number of men who find it nearly impossible to let go of arguments with women, I suggest that this lore is faulty, and the tendency to cogitate over arguments may be more widespread in men than is thought. I'm optimistic that as men learn to access and talk about their feelings, better ways to bridge the gap will be found.

As I've learned from many men and their frustrated partners, the reality is that when arguments flare up and don't get resolved, men frequently shut down, sometimes for weeks before talking about the issue with their partners again. I'm unclear whether this is martyr behavior or simply the inability to resolve issues fairly and quickly. But I am convinced that a couple's lack of problem resolution skills leads to this brand of dysfunctional behavior. The notion of getting into bed every night for weeks on end, angry, frustrated, and unable or unwilling to talk through a problem is anathema to the men in my group. Peter was the exception.

I can't imagine remaining in that dead, loveless space for longer than it takes for someone to simply admit they were wrong, and move on. I asked Peter what seemed like an obvious question, "Peter, I'm assuming you feel hurt when that occurs. Have you ever told your wife that it hurts your feelings when she recites her laundry list to you?"

He replied, "Yeah, I do feel hurt, and you know, I never thought to say that to her. So no, I haven't ever told her it hurts my feelings. Maybe I will the next time this happens."

The next time we met, Peter mentioned that his wife's laundry list had come up again, but this time he'd responded differently. "I told her it hurt my feelings when she does this, and that she does it so often that I walk around angry much of our time together. But the truth is that I'm really hurt and I can't just hug and forgive her." Peter paused and added, "She did say she was sorry." If this particular story had a happy ending, this might have been a major turning point in Peter's relationship.

Sadly, since Peter's marriage lacked any foundation for trust, this issue kept rearing its ugly head. Peter's late-blooming, emotional honesty skills weren't enough to overcome their years of destructive exchanges. While his story may seem like a somber example deserving a discussion about what's in it for all of us, it is a lesson—in what to avoid. Why choose dysfunction when a relationship can be positive and loving? Think how much better it is to start dating with honesty, protect the relationship from the inevitable damage from dysfunctional behavior, and continue exchanging emotionally honest feelings with each other.

Everyone deserve to be in a relationship that embraces emotional honesty from the very first date, and a little patience around how it's delivered can go a long way towards having a satisfying dialogue. A relationship that embraces emotional honesty has a chance of success, while a relationship that doesn't has no chance at all. Accepting a man who's working to become more skilled in this arena, will encourage him to continue doing this work and vice versa. A man or woman who is able to share how their feelings about each other and their relationship, will likely result in both getting what they want and need from each other. They'll be able to understand each other's needs, since both spoke from their hearts, and not just their heads (or libidos). This is a carefully choreographed dance that partners can learn and improve upon over time. The most vital factor is a mutual willingness to expose their deepest feelings, trusting that those feelings will be respected and honored.

Nothing matters more developing a relationship than deepening the intimacy, and expressing honest feelings as they arise allows room for intimacy to grow. A friend calls this keeping it clean, which means not allowing bad feelings to go unexpressed, because eventually the held back feelings explode, and then any resolution becomes more difficult. Confronting issues quickly in a relationship, rather than allowing them to fester, is key. This is the moment of truth for couples, when it's possible to work those issues out and maintain feelings of love.

In many relationships, men and women demonstrate patience, caring, and kindness, fairly evenly. The gender gap between boomer men and women can be narrowed if not eliminated, by the expression and acknowledgement of each other's feelings. While that's not always easy, it is within the reach of most boomers, men and women. Boomers have been through a lot of emotionally trying experiences, and even if we don't all have the best skills regarding emotionally honest dialogue yet, we can develop our skills by practicing it in our relationships and in every aspect of our lives.

Chapter Five:
Ready to Date

What is a broken heart?

A broken heart sounds like a medical condition for which there's no cure. Broken suggests something in the realm of trying to put Humpty Dumpty back together again, which every child knows is an impossible feat. But a broken heart after a failed relationship is absolutely reparable, and a healed heart is literally as good as new. Perhaps a more fitting name would be a 'bruised' heart, but 'bruised' lacks the devastation of 'broken'. The bruising I'm referring to feels like physical pain, a kind of dull ache that suggests someone reaching into your chest, pulling your heart out, slapping it around for a while, and then jamming it back into your body. Unlike physical pain, which usually diminishes on its own over time, the dull ache of a heartbreak lingers, and the longer the pain remains ignored, in terms of not doing the work to heal it, the longer it hurts.

The extreme example of lingering pain occurs when someone ignores their heartbreak entirely, and is puzzled each time, their pain surfaces again. I've met many melancholy people who are stuck in past, failed relationships. It doesn't take much conversation to realize why they've never healed after listening to them pour out their hearts. Just ask a man or woman stuck in heartbreak denial about the partner or relationship that inflicted the wound, and the anger and/or tears flow as if the break-up occurred yesterday. Perhaps the lamest bromide of all is that time heals all wounds. No, it doesn't, because emotional wounds that go untended never heal, no matter how much time goes by. The heartbreak demons lurk in our psyches and pop up without warning. They're as sticky as glue, and they have all the time you choose to give them to inflict pain.

Someone who breaks a leg skiing knows without having to ask a doctor, or anyone else for that matter, that getting back on the slopes before their leg is perfectly healed is a recipe for disaster. However, the same man or woman may think nothing of dating immediately following a heart-wrenching break-up. They blithely forge ahead with reckless abandon as if nothing happened, ignoring the fact that the damage done to their heart needs to be healed to the same degree as the damage to their leg. Rather than waiting until their heart is healed, they take it out for a spin, hoping that dating will magically make the pain go away, or that a new love will somehow absorb their pain. This degree of naiveté takes denial to new heights.

What I know about healing with absolute certainty is that no one can move on until the pain from a broken heart is healed, and that can only be accomplished through the grieving process. Unless someone is totally unconscious, and lacks the ability to feel their own pain, skipping the healing process guaranties that the pain that will surface, get stuffed down, and resurface, ad infinitum. We've all met men and women who are still filled with anger and bitterness long after the end of a relationship. It's all but certain that these folks skipped the healing process. They're stuck in a cycle of anger, sadness, and pain, and will remain stuck for as long as they ignore their broken hearts. This is myopic, unconscious behavior, since dating shortly after a long-term relationship break-up can't possibly lead to a successful relationship, until the pain is resolved.

Does this mean that a man or woman can't date until they grieve the loss of a partner and the relationship? No, but any conscious person will recognize a date who's still hurting and emotionally stuck in their last relationship and the smart ones will walk away before they're relegated to the role of victim to that person's unresolved pain. The worst date I can recall was with a woman who had skipped the healing process, and who was so filled with vitriol that she could barely contain it. Our coffee date quickly turned into a volcano of anger directed at men, including me. Her comment that men treat middle-aged women as if they're disposable didn't resonate with me, especially when I discovered that her heartbreak was in its second year. Even though I was in my early forties, and hadn't learned much about the healing process yet, I knew instinctively that her behavior was way out of bounds. I told her so and ended our date.

Recognizing that a failed, long-term relationship is an emotional death should make it abundantly clear why the healing process is critical. While there are five traditional stages of grieving loss after a death, a few in particular apply to healing a broken heart after a breakup. Denial may be an aspect of a broken heart, particularly if someone got blindsided, taken completely by surprise by the abrupt end of a relationship. Feeling you're in a loving relationship and having your partner tell you the relationship is over, or that they met someone else, falls into the denial category. A relationship that was in trouble for a while doesn't typically end up in the denial category, because both partners had ample time to prepare for the breakup. Still, sometimes getting blindsided can't be avoided.

Anger may be the most difficult phase of grieving to process, in part because it's the first stage. When betrayal is the suspect in a breakup, anger can reach over-the-top status. Some broken-hearted people also feel depressed for a while. Acceptance, the final stage of grieving, allows broken-hearted people to finally heal and move on. Dating before healing is a sure-fire way to become one of the walking wounded date zombies. In addition, you'll also be the worst possible date.

A Rush to Oblivion

My own unfailingly, unrealistic, quack cure for a broken heart after a break-up, was to jump into the next relationship as quickly as I could find someone to date. I practiced this ill-fated, get back on your horse immediately after you're thrown philosophy of non-recovery, for many years before I woke up to the reality that I needed to heal first. Even though every one of my relationships ultimately failed, I still felt reasonably confident I was a smart guy for not wasting time feeling sorry for myself. Real men don't feel sorry for themselves, do they?

Was my unbelievably unconscious, post break-up behavior an anomaly? Sadly it wasn't. It was almost predictable and in fact was solidly mainstream, male post-break-up behavior. When I think back on how I probably came across to women, I'm surprised any dated me. It wasn't difficult to notice I was stuck in a bad place. The only viable reason that any woman dated me is that most, if not all, the other available men I competed with for dates, were equally lost and in denial about healing before dating again, and that women just didn't have many better choices. Or perhaps women's previous experiences with men indicated that dating unhealed zombies, who expected them to provide some amount of healing, was normal. I'm fairly certain that I was a heavy emotional burden. Mea culpa.

I'm coaching a boomer woman friend with online dating. She recently asked me why men seemed to buzz so glibly from one relationship to the next without a moment's pause. I knew the answer, but I stalled for a few moments because I was ashamed of what she'd labeled men's buzzing behavior, and I was trying to think how to sugar coat it. But I couldn't conjure up any way to mask the truth. So I told her what I know about men jumping from one relationship to the next, I learned from working with men for a quarter century, my own dating experiences, and thousands of comments from readers. In truth, a surprising number of men think that behavior is normal for a guy, and that there's nothing wrong with behaving normally, right? Men may put a Band-Aid on their broken hearts by acknowledging that they're feeling badly, but many truly believe that the best way to heal it is simply to find a new woman and fall in love again. Who says men aren't romantic and resourceful?

I've also dated women I met online who were a month or less out of their last long-term relationship, and as is the case with unhealed men, they believed that getting involved again quickly was the panacea for their pain. Incredibly, one was a psychotherapist who mentioned ten minutes into our coffee date that she felt this date might be a mistake. When I asked why, she said she'd only broken up with her live-in boyfriend of seven years two weeks before. I couldn't resist asking her why she didn't know better, considering that she counsels people about this issue. She sat quietly, stared into her coffee, and didn't answer. I thanked her and left.

Another online, unhealed date from Hell remains forever stuck in my memory. We met for a coffee date, and the moment she sat down she began a ten-minute, non-stop tirade about her dirt bag ex-husband and his effin lawyer. She barely breathed between vitriol- punctuated sentences, and she was oblivious to how a total stranger might feel listening to her. I wondered if she'd agreed to our date because she just wanted a man on whom she could vent her anger. When she finally stopped, she was literally out of breath and in a deeply agitated state. I thanked her for meeting me, and left. I didn't feel obligated to continue in my conscripted role as her personal piñata.

You're Not God's Gift if You're Still Hurting

There are lots of faux pas that boomers can commit when dating, and my experience suggests that the most egregious is showing up for a date while still recovering from a past relationship. I learned this lesson the hard way. When I was in my early forties, I made a date with a woman a week after I'd broken up with a girlfriend. I was sure that getting back on the horse was my best move, and the notion of working through my pain never even dawned on me. We talked for a few minutes, and I can still remember clearly that I was unable to make eye contact with her.

Still, I was startled when she looked at me like I'd eaten the frosting off her cupcake. I felt as if she was x-raying my psyche and stripping my soul naked. She maintained eye contact, which I felt obligated to meet, albeit with extreme difficulty. She never blinked when she asked how long it had been since my last relationship.

When I told her a week, she scolded me sarcastically, "Call me in a year when you're over it." Then she got up and left the café without ever looking back. If she had she would have noticed I wore a look of humiliation on my face. I realized in that moment that she was right about me, and I felt like the most unconscious jerk on the planet. I'd made a date with an attractive, interesting woman while I was still hurting from a previous relationship, and that level of ignorance didn't make me feel proud of myself as a man.

That was the first time a woman had ever been so bluntly direct with me, and when I finally recovered from the humiliation, I surrendered to the truth. I'd ignored all of my feelings about everything far too long, and it was clear that I wasn't going to get away with that delusional behavior any longer. Getting older and continuing to date age-appropriate women meant that my behavior was transparent to women. Most saw right through me. I wised up after discovering that no matter how well I dressed or was groomed, I wouldn't be attractive to any woman who knew what to look for, particularly if she didn't want the job of being her date's therapist. I was an emotional train wreck, and I was ashamed of how I'd behaved with women. She had pointed out the path I'd managed to ignore, and her wake-up call saved me further humiliation and failure. I was grateful she'd pointed out my dysfunctional behavior. She was kind to do so, even though our date ended with, good luck and good-bye. I felt relieved but didn't have a clue what to do next.

Healing Shows Strength, Not Weakness

I regret having to be brutally honest about pointing out the usual suspects who generally fail to heal their pain before dating again, but it's nearly always men that skip the post break-up healing process. Men are far more likely than women to jump from one relationship into the next without pause, and some choose to invoke a primal explanation for their propensity to buzz. "It's in our male DNA to procreate with as many women as possible." While that was true thousands of years ago, it has absolutely no basis in fact today. It's a poor excuse for remaining emotionally brain dead, and I doubt there's a woman alive who buys into it.

I have women friends who've spent a year or two grieving failed relationships, in order to recover before dating again. They hang out with friends and spend time alone working through their pain. Dating just isn't on their radar screens. I admire their discipline and dedication to healing and becoming emotionally healthy again, but I doubt they spend their time healing just to be good dates for men. It's more likely they do it to feel good about themselves again. That's the chasm that separates between boomer men and women. It's the difference between how the genders process, or don't process, emotional pain. Thousands of comments from boomer women indicate this is a serious dating stumbling block. I'll take them at their word, and I suggest other men do the same.

Most boomer women have done some amount of inner or personal growth work. Dating is one arena in particular that the gender difference regarding working or not working through hurt feelings is obvious. Boomer women don't want to become involved in relationships with men who ignore their pain, because they're aware that it's likely that those men won't be able to feel their pain either. They expect and deserve a peer partner and that means one who has done sufficient inner work to recognize that healing between relationships is a given, not optional.

It's a Guy Thing

Since few boomer boys were taught to talk about their feelings, many are incapable of that dialogue as men. In addition to not being able to share how they're feeling, because getting in touch with their feelings isn't second nature for most men, fewer still are willing to share their feelings with anyone, anyway. It's unmanly and wimpy for a guy to talk about his feelings, right? For boomer men who still struggle to get in touch with, and express their feelings, or haven't ever tried, this is a wake-up call. There are no successful relationships that don't include dialogue regarding how each partner is feeling about each other and the relationship. It's a fantasy to think otherwise, just as it is to think unresolved problems won't eventually end a relationship. The good news is that there's no age limit for doing this inner work.

Guys, when you break up with a woman after a long-term relationship, it's not the next woman's job to heal your pain and make you feel better, or to dig your relationship history out of you either. Your emotional health is your responsibility, and it's naive and disrespectful to think otherwise. You're responsible for doing the work involved to get past your pain after a broken relationship, but first you have to know how to access that pain. That hurt doesn't live in your head, no matter how much you think about it. Your pain resides solely in your heart. Ouch, I know that's not a place lots of guys feel comfortable going, but there's nowhere else to find it. Getting this right can feel like an enormous relief after ignoring your feelings for a long time. Becoming conscious and capable of talking about your emotions will diminish the amount of strife in your next relationship.

Strength in Numbers

When I was forty, and still in the throes of working through my emotional issues alone, because I didn't have any men friends, I decided to change my status as a lone wolf. I got seven other guys together at my home to talk one evening. I only knew one fellow, but he knew another, and so on. It took a less than a week to schedule this meeting. The first decision this fledgling group made was that what was said in the room would stay in the room. The second was that rather than giving each other advice, which is the typical dialogue between men, we'd share our emotional experiences in similar situations that other men brought up instead. We would offer what we did in their situations that worked and what didn't work. This was a major eye-opener for most of us, and while we had to learn to trust each other as part of the experiential sharing, this was the beginning of my men's group twenty-five years ago.

Men can either choose to be their own worst enemies or they can choose to be their own best friends. Leaving his ego behind allows a man to be open and honest with other men about his issues, and the biggest issue after twenty-five years that still comes up nearly every time we meet, is relationships. We all want to get it right with women, but not all of us have the skills to make that happen. Men can teach each other the lessons about accessing and discussing feelings in a manner that few of us learned as boys. When I told my guys the story about the woman with the x-ray eyes, whose comments shoved me onto a better path, they all smiled, remembering their dating disasters with women.

Women and Friendships

I can't state the reasons why women seem more prone to resolve their post relationship pain than men with absolute certainty, but I've noticed one factor in particular that seems to contribute to women's ability to do the healing work. Most women have a tight knit circle of women friends they've known for decades or longer. In their time together, they've developed unconditional trust, and learned the healing value derived from sharing their issues with each other.

Women began meeting together in groups at the start of the sixties, and the women who worked together to achieve their goals locally, fueled the national Women's Movement. Their stamina, determination, and passion for equal rights were inexhaustible. Are women more emotional than men? Perhaps, but what seems far more relevant, in terms of boomer dating, is that women are more *connected* with their emotions than men.

Men couldn't help but notice what women were achieving working together, but they mostly ignored the process that led to women's successes. While it was okay for women, real men kept their troubles to themselves, didn't they? A few men drummed in the woods and told each other heroic fables. Ant that was pretty much the extent of the men's movement in the sixties. However, a small number of men did begin meeting together. I live in the Bay Area of San Francisco, where forward thinking people are supposedly in abundance, but I only know a few men who meet with other men to talk about the issues they're struggling with. It's time for men to wake up to the possibilities, and teach each other the lessons that actually make men stronger. Being a loner is like living in a vacuum, where there's no oxygen, and nothing grows. No smart woman dates a loner, because she knows she'll become his entire universe by default. It takes enormous strength for a man to talk with other men, even with unconditional trust, but that's the nature of authentic friendships.

I look forward to getting together with my guy friends to talk about sports, movies, travel, and a myriad of other topics that my men's group doesn't talk about. That kind of camaraderie is good for men, and on some basis serves as a bonding tool. But it's also just surface stuff, and that dialogue ignores the issues that men struggle with. Men can have both of those types of relationships with other men. I've never met a woman who didn't appreciate a man who had men friends with whom he could work through his issues. When I mentioned to women that I was in a men's group, I went to the head of their line.

Who You Calling a Wimp?

When I first started writing for *The Huffington Post,* I mentioned the intrinsic value of men talking about their issues together. Several fellows suggested that men who do are wimpy. Come on guys, honestly? In your heart of hearts do you actually believe that stuffing your feelings down every day is an intelligent or effective way to deal with your issues? Do you really believe that you can actually make those feelings disappear just because you stuffed them down? Haven't you heard of the carnival game, Whack a Mole? Every time you bury a painful feeling it's guaranteed to resurface until you do the work to put it to rest. Do you believe that remaining a tough guy loner will in some manner help you meet a sweet, compassionate woman to date and create a relationship with?

Whether or not you're ready to date after a failed relationship isn't debatable. If you're still feeling hurt or anxious from your last relationship, then you're not ready to date, and if you think about that relationship most of the day, you're not ready to date either. When you remember the person you were in relationship with, and anger is the feeling that surfaces, you're not ready to date. If you ignore the obvious you'll suffer self-inflicted wounds, and you'll also hurt the poor soul who unknowingly agrees to date you. Healing before dating again is a universal, unconditional rule that boomers either know, or need to learn. Dating is difficult enough under the best of circumstances. Respect yourself and the women you date. Becoming the best possible date, and future partner of someone special, depends on it. Keeping in mind that you'll be expected to give as good as you get in a relationship, are you capable of bringing your best?

If you drag an unsuspecting woman into a relationship when you're rebounding, you'll be harming that woman beyond what's reasonable or acceptable. No one should be considered fodder for your anger or pain. Being clear-headed and openhearted about where you are in your emotional process, as regards healing from a failed relationship is critical. Ignoring the healing process and dating, is a hostile act no woman will thank you for. You can't open your heart to someone new if you're still feeling the sting from your last relationship.

Chapter Six:
An Introduction to Online Dating

Pick a Path

Single boomers have to get real if they hope to ever meet the love of their lives. And getting real doesn't mean hoping you'll bump into the love of your life in a park or supermarket. The odds that you'll magically cross paths with someone the appropriate age, height, body type, marital status, personality, recreational interests, and emotional intelligence, are so remote that your continued single status is all but guaranteed. Hope is not a dating strategy. Like everything worthwhile in life, dating requires effort and energy.

Sticky Stuff

There are times when the online dating process may feel like trying to swim through molasses. Any boomer can become weary and wary after trying to determine which members, out of the hundreds or thousands available on a dating site, to send invitations, and which invitations received, to accept. The line between who's acceptable and who's not, can quickly become blurred after thirty minutes staring at your computer screen, scrolling through profiles. Maintaining the resolve required to meet your life partner takes equal amounts of grit, determination, and stamina. Is the reward worth what sometimes feels like pushing a boulder up a hill? For most boomers it is, because no matter how many good friends a boomer has, or how close they are with their adult children and grandchildren, most recognize that these aren't substitutes for being in a sweet relationship for decades to come.

Honoring Lost Love

The Scoville Scale, invented in 1912, measures the degree of heat in peppers. It's a helpful guide, because it tells users how to choose peppers that are appropriately hot for them. There's no chart that measures the degree of grief a widow or widower is feeling. No one can advise a man or woman who has lost a partner, how long it takes to heal, or when it's appropriate to date. Widows and widowers have told me many times that their relationships with their deceased spouses were so incredible, that no one could possibly measure up, so what's the point of dating? Some feel that dating would be disrespectful to their lost loved one, so they remain single and alone. While I respect their sentiments, I think they may be missing an important aspect about dating that's worth considering. Creating a friendship, and maybe a partnership with a new love, can enhance the joy in a widow/widower's life, and provide a loving and supportive relationship. No one can take a lost loved one's place, nor should anyone try, or be expected to. That isn't the point of dating after a loss, and it's important not to think of a new love interest as someone who has to compete with a lost husband or wife. An openhearted attitude allows room for something unique, different, and fulfilling to develop.

With decades left to live, there's so much joy still to be shared with someone special to treat you in the caring and respectful manner you deserve. The grief of losing a loved one leaves an empty space that feels like it can't ever be filled again. In some ways it can't, because unlike a boomer recovering from a divorce, a death is a more painful loss, because the survivor didn't voluntarily separate from their life partner. It seems doubtful a loving spouse would want his or her surviving partner to grieve them to the exclusion of any possible happiness in the future. If you're a widow or widower, you may have already come to this conclusion since you're reading a dating book. Please allow yourself to feel okay about reaching out to other single boomers. There's no disrespect in it, but there *is* the potential for a wonderful surprise. I wish you good luck, and I hope you find someone who makes you feel alive and warm in your heart again.

What Will It Take To Meet The Love Of Your Life?

It's your thoughtful, creative, energetic approach to online dating that will ensure your success, not luck, and you're going to have to be proactive to succeed. Waiting passively for your online dating website mailbox to fill up is reactive, and that type of passivity significantly reduces your chances. Take a bold, proactive stance instead. Contact potential dates and announce your interest and availability.

It's disappointing and frustrating to send an invitation to someone you're interested in and not get a response, but one of the realities of online dating is that no one is everyone's cup of tea. It's helpful not to build any fantasies around someone you contacted, at least until you actually meet in person. Also, keep in mind that this type of online dating rejection isn't personal. Everyone online is a stranger and I don't believe anyone intentionally hurts another member's feelings by not responding to an email invitation. Most online daters feel that explaining why they're not interested in dating someone is unnecessary, and I agree. If your invitation to someone you contacted is ignored, move on and contact other potential dates.

A woman friend always assumes she wrote an inappropriate email invitation if she doesn't get a response from the man she contacted. I remind her that clicking with someone, particularly online, isn't an everyday occurrence, and that even people who probably should meet, don't always. Online dating requires a somewhat thick skin, in terms of not taking rejection personally. It also takes courage and determination to jump back into the dating pool after feeling disappointed. But online dating works for so many people that it's worth enduring the occasional, inevitable, harsh feelings. While finding your life partner isn't going to be easy, it isn't remotely like finding a needle in a haystack.

Never Forget

The person you're looking for is looking for you too, and they're as frustrated and fatigued as you are. The joy of meeting your life partner is exhilarating, in part because the grueling search is finally over. Nut making your worlds collide only happens if you don't give up.

Friends Mean Well

When you first began dating after a long-term relationship, it probably didn't take long to exhaust your friends' short lists of single friends. While everyone likes the idea of introducing people, they'll likely introduce you to every single friend, your personal criteria notwithstanding. Even though your friends have the best intentions and want to help you, in the end, you're going to have to rely on your own efforts.

The Elusive Brass Ring

Even if you acknowledge that finding your life partner is ultimately your responsibility, you may still feel hopelessly lost in the boomer, dating maze. If you're recently single, dating is far more complicated today than what you remember when you last dated. Most boomers out of long-term relationships have raised children, had careers, and built lifelong friendships. Your life feels settled, and you're pleased by how it turned out. But you may feel lonely, especially if all of your friends are partnered. Don't worry because dating isn't like musical chairs. There are still plenty of terrific single boomers left.

Consider that your criteria for a partner are very different than when you were younger. Your friends, family, pets, activities, interests, passions, and just about everything else in your life can be shared with a new partner. Hopefully, your next partner has a life that's as complete as yours. The blending of two, joyful lives, is rich beyond measure.

What's critical is that the man or woman you're looking for is principled, embodies integrity, and has an emotional vocabulary, because all three will be needed to smooth out the relationship rough spots that will surely occur. As every salesperson quickly discovers, you get what you aim for, in business, and choosing dates. Aim high and don't ever settle for less. While the available number of perfect life partner choices may be limited, the trick is being able to pick that person out of the crowd. Online dating saves a lot of time and effort if you don't waste time going out with inappropriate people. Focus.

Gender Angst

When I began dating online a while ago, I was surprised to discover a gender gap that I didn't remember when I'd dated years before. Some of the rift is related to boomer women's lack of interest in casual sex. But there's more that keeps boomer men and women at loggerheads. Our expectations are frequently different, which means that a number of dating boomers are likely to be disappointed. And even a small number of disappointments can spark anger and hostility, and discourage the desire to continuing dating.

Most boomer women think about dating in the context of finding a partner who has qualities their ex's likely didn't. After a failed long-term relationship, many women want to find a partner with an emotional IQ, problem resolution skills, and a willingness to commit. Since the first two qualities may have been sketchy or missing in a previous relationship, they're non-negotiable now. Absent meeting a man who has these qualities, based on thousands of comments from readers, the majority of boomer women prefer to put sex and dating on hold rather than continue struggling dating boomer guys.. I know quite a few boomer women who fit this category, and frankly, they seem to be living full, enjoyable lives. That doesn't mean they wouldn't like to meet a man who meets their parameters, but most aren't optimistic about finding him.

Casual sex is certainly a major source of some of the gender conflict, and it shouldn't be much of a stretch for a man to understand how a boomer woman might feel about being expected to sexually satisfy a stranger on a first date. Since casual sex rarely develops into to a long-term relationship, and more often ends in disappointment, their position makes sense. It's demeaning and dismissive for men to treat women in this manner, and every boomer guy knows it is whether he appreciates the reality of this truth or not. Boomer women have earned our respect.

Having said this, I realize that some boomer men, and a smaller number of boomer women, just want to date to have sex. While I have no moral judgment about that, I feel this needs to be mentioned even before the first date, perhaps in a phone conversation. It may feel awkward, but that's the point, isn't it? It's better to turn a woman off and away from you because of your first date sexual preference, than to waste her time and cause undue stress on the actual date. There are boomer men and women who still feel casual sex is viable, but my experience and those of the men and women who comment on my articles, is that they're a small minority of single dating boomers. There's no need for pretense or deception, because that's a road leading nowhere. So if what you really want is just sex, and maybe a relationship afterward, being honest about that up front will spare you and your date undue conflict.

This isn't an insurmountable gap for boomer men and women to close. No matter the nature of the conflict, or the different approaches to dating, nearly every boomer man and woman is dating to find love. It's what that love looks like that sometimes divides us. We all know boomer couples that met, fell in love, and are living happily ever after, and while we're encouraged by their success stories, we can easily become discouraged after experiencing several false starts. But we persist in our search because the reward is so enticing. This chapter is a roadmap for finding love, and if you follow it your chances will increase exponentially.

There are avenues where single boomers can meet besides online dating, and I'll suggest a few later in this chapter. However, there are far too many success stories coming out of the online dating community to ignore it as a valuable resource, and since online dating is rapidly becoming the most popular method for boomers to meet, it shouldn't be dismissed out of hand. I've heard from many boomers, women in particular, who have given up online dating. While it can be frustrating, my pointers can take a lot of the sting out of the process and help smooth over the pain from past mistakes. Giving up isn't an option unless you're resigned to being alone.

Deciding which site(s) to join is the first online dating hurdle. There are many, and new ones seem to pop up like weeds monthly. Some websites charge monthly fees while others are free. My extensive online dating experience suggests that the quality and quantity of available dates isn't necessarily linked to cost. I'll share more about these sites further in this chapter but it's worth mentioning that I met the love of my life on a boomer dating website. I suggest joining a few sites as a smart strategy to cover your bases and, while you'll run across some of the same people on different sites, you'll find many you wouldn't have otherwise. Some boomer dating sites have affiliates, which means that if you belong to one you're automatically on both.

Nearly all boomer, dating websites have made using their sites easier, but there's a safety factor to consider before joining a dating website and I'll share how to mitigate some of the safety issues that plague online dating.

Not a Frog Kissing Contest

The key to successful online dating is developing the ability to recognize that while there may be hundreds, or even thousands, of potential date choices that fit your age bracket, picking appropriate dates isn't throwing darts at those choices, and conversely, it isn't shooting fish in a barrel either. Choosing dates at random is a shotgun approach guaranteed to waste your time and frustrate you, and eventually convince you that online dating doesn't work.

Success requires technique because online dating isn't a total gamble. If you feel you're kissing too many frogs, your technique may need improvement, because smart online dating isn't a numbers game. When someone insists the trick to meeting a special person is to go out on lots of dates until you do, they're demonstrating a lack of dating expertise. Focus determines success, and that means zeroing in on exactly the person you're looking for. You'll waste an incredible opportunity if you stray from your target. Is compatibility important? Sure, to some extent, but while a relationship that has the legs to endure for decades may include compatibility, it isn't nearly a good enough reason to become involved with someone. You'll shortchange yourself by accepting compatibility as a rationale for a relationship, because there's so much that matters even more.

My articles in *The Huffington Post* and *AARP* have garnered comments from men and women in fairly equal percentages, but it's boomer women who complain the most about online dating frustrations. Many insist that the available boomer men don't meet their minimum standards, or that all the good men are taken. They contend that the available men are arrogant, because they know that women online greatly outnumber them. I strongly suggest to men that arrogance, or anything less than good manners and politeness, is shortsighted. If you live in an area where women greatly outnumber men online, consider your numerical edge in a positive light in terms of having lots of good choices, instead of as an excuse for bad manners. I urge boomer women to consider that all of the good men are not taken, and that finding yours will be easier if you follow the suggestions in this chapter.

My intention for writing this chapter is to improve the quality of your online dating experience and make it more fruitful and enjoyable. Having found love online altered my life immeasurably, and I'd like every boomer man or woman to enjoy a similar level of success. Luck is always helpful, but it wasn't the main reason my partner and I met. We were both proactive about meeting someone special, and we both endured a plethora of dull coffee dates before we finally did. We definitely became discouraged at times, but neither of us considered giving up. The stakes were too high to quit. My suggestions are based entirely on my online dating experiences, and those of men and women who have commented on my dating and relationship articles in *The Huffington Post* and *AARP*.

Step One: Post an Attractive Photo

A boomer needs to consider his or her online dating profile as their personal menu, and their photo is the first item anyone will notice on that menu. It's what catches everyone's initial attention, and its quality frequently determines whether or not other singles bother reading the profile that follows. I've never seen a restaurant feature liver and onions at the top of its menu. Instead, they feature a dish that's attractive, appealing, and representative of their creative efforts. Your profile photo should be similarly appealing and reflect your best efforts. Anything less is a waste of a near perfect opportunity to meet your next partner.

It always surprises me when I see a woman's profile photo featuring a gloomy face, wearing large sunglasses, a big floppy hat, in shadows, lost in a group shot, or taken at a distance. The results are predictably bad. I've also seen women post driver's license photos, even though they resemble mug shots. There's only thing worse than posting a bad photo, and that's not posting any photo, which is a major mistake, and absolutely guaranteed to fail to produce a date. Who is going to bother reading a profile featuring a website's silhouette icon in place of a photo? Practically no one, and you've effectively reduced your chances of meeting someone to nearly zero. The lack of a photo automatically suggests someone unattractive, not fully engaged, painfully shy, or married, none of which will encourage anyone to dig deeper. Unless you're married and don't want your husband or wife's friends to recognize you, for heaven's sake, post a decent photo.

A large number of women have shared that men are equally photo challenged so I took a look at men's online photos. I have to concur that a lot of guys are making the same mistakes. As I skipped over profiles featuring unappealing photos, I wondered if the posters were truly serious about dating. I also wondered if the people who don't post any photo harbor a secret fantasy that their one true love will see beyond the blank space where their photo should be, and magically choose them. It's every serious dater's responsibility to put his or her best foot forward, and posting an appealing photo is the minimum effort.

A woman friend's profile photo showed her sitting in the front seat of her car looking out the driver's side window, holding her dog on her lap. It looked like she was ordering at the drive through at a fast food restaurant. Not surprisingly, her profile hadn't gotten many clicks. We posted better photos and her email inbox began to fill up. Is it really that simple? Yeah, sometimes it is, because making it as easy as possible for someone to choose you begins with posting an attractive photo.

The same woman friend called me for advice right before I finished this chapter. She'd met a guy online. She liked what he had to say about himself, but couldn't help notice that two of his three photos showed his face pressed against women's faces. When she talked with him she asked about the women in his photos, since a relationship of some sort seemed probable. He hemmed and hawed for a while, but when she pressed him, he mentioned that they were women he had been in relationships with. She was flabbergasted that he chose to post photos with old girlfriends. She passed after realizing she couldn't get her arms around the mindset of a guy who posted photos with old girlfriends. While it feels odd to have to say this, it's entirely inappropriate to post photos with old girlfriends.

Make posting a good photo simple. Ask a friend to take some shots. A headshot is okay as your main photo, but you'll also need a full-length shot. Online daters want to see your entire physical appearance, so your photos should represent you accurately. Here's the key to posting a winning photo. The single most attractive feature in any man or woman's photo is their smile. A smiling face is automatically attractive because it suggests happiness, a positive outlook on life, and good self-esteem.

Beyond a smiling face and a full-length shot, feel free to include photos of your children, grandchildren, dog, cat, car, boat, or motorcycle. Just remember no sunglasses, big hats, baseball caps, or group shots. And I repeat, smile because it's critical, and I assure you it will catch everyone's attention. Whether it's fair or not, people read a lot into a photo, and a sour face suggests a depressed or angry person. Think of the funniest thing you ever saw or heard and smile accordingly when the camera clicks.

Huge Photo Mistakes

There's no need to hire a professional photographer. Besides the cost, professional photos typically look staged or airbrushed, which isn't necessarily appealing. The single most egregious reported photo offense that generates the most vitriolic comments from daters is people posting old photos. I've heard numerous stories from both men and women about how they didn't recognize their dates in person because their online photos were so old. Posting photos a few years old or older is dishonest, period. The notion that the right man or woman will appreciate the real you in person, after you've misrepresented yourself, is naive because none will appreciate that you've intentionally misled them.

A woman wrote to me about her experience with a first date whose online photo featured a forty-something guy, in shape, clean-shaven and with a full head of wavy brown hair. As you've probably guessed, the man who sat down at her table in the café literally shocked her. He was fifty-something, fat, bearded, and bald. She was furious. She got up and stood over the imposter, but just long enough to ask what had possessed him to post such an ancient photo. His answer, "Because I love that old picture of myself." She was speechless, and she left him to his fantasies. Wasting someone's time in this manner is disrespectful, and is one of the reasons a first date should always be a coffee date, in a very public cafe during the day. You can walk out if necessary, which you have every right to do if your date has been dishonest.

Another Reason to Exit

There are other reasons that warrant walking out on a coffee date, and perhaps the most common is a date that talks endlessly about his or her ex. I remember one woman I met for coffee several years ago. She was stunningly beautiful, but after a brief introduction she couldn't stop talking about her ex-husband. She was livid, and she may have had a right to be, but clearly wasn't ready to date. I thanked her for coming and left. Showing up for a date means more than being physically present. It also means being emotionally healthy and healed from your last relationship. This isn't something a date can help with, so do the work before wasting a good opportunity, and someone else's time.

The Truth and Nothing But the Truth

The notion that it's acceptable to lie about your age in your profile because everyone else does, always seemed like total nonsense to me. While it's true that quite a few men and women fudge their ages, I feel that being dishonest about anything is a red flag. It's also foolish since the truth will emerge soon enough, and using the lame excuse that everyone else does it won't mitigate the lie. Trust is a major factor in a relationship, and trust is defined by integrity. For heaven's sake, be honest. If nothing else, it's refreshing.

If you believe you have to lie because you're too old to date successfully online without lying, you probably are, but it's your unwillingness to be honest that's the problem, not your age. Behaving as if it's okay to be dishonest because lots of other people are is the kind of nonsense your parents turned around on you when they asked if you'd jump off a bridge if your friends did. Instead of dissembling about your age, make a positive statement about it. Express that you're proud of it, and that it has neither slowed you down nor jaded your enthusiasm for love or life. Sure, some men and women will skip past your profile, but not the ones you want to attract, who are far more interested in your personality than your chronology. I know this may sound like something that only works in a perfect world, but there are plenty of singles that want to meet someone close to their age.

Step Two: Write a Creative Profile

The second important step for meeting the love of your life online is to write a compelling, creative profile that will intrigue and motivate an absolute stranger, sufficient to want to contact you. This involves more work than your photo, because writing a winning profile requires some creative thought. With the exception of income, it's an enormous mistake to check the boxes indicating, I'll tell you later, instead of sharing your information. It comes across as thinly veiled arrogance, and suggests a lack of interest in the dating process, or laziness, neither of which are appealing qualities. If you treat your profile like an afterthought, your chances will be greatly reduced. Like it or not, online dating is competitive, and if you fail to post a creative profile to accompany your smiling photo, you already lost to the men and women that did.

It's shortsighted and shallow to think your good looks alone are sufficient to attract the right kind of attention. That attitude will only attract other shallow people that choose dates based solely on looks. You're either seriously interested in meeting someone appropriate or you're wasting your time. As boomers, we don't have time to waste in relationships that last only as long as good looks alone can ensure. Sure, boomers are resilient, but what's the point of getting embroiled in a never-ending series of brief, unconscious entanglements with inappropriate people?

Writing a great online profile requires some measure of writing skill. If you feel yours are lacking, ask a friend or co-worker who writes well to help you. Spelling mistakes and grammatical errors are unnecessary and unforgivable. While standing out is the point, you don't want to stand out for the wrong reasons. No one ever picked anyone whose profile suggested they were borderline illiterate. I've helped several friends write their profiles. It's not a big deal to ask a friend for help.

Writing a surefire profile doesn't mean including everything that ever happened in your life. Some information, like family history, is better discovered in person over time. A profile that wanders aimlessly and endlessly gets passed, because few people are willing to wade through a lot of unfocused information. Less is more when it's creatively written. For instance, it may appear more like boasting than sharing if you list every country you've ever visited. Instead, pick a favorite and write a screenplay for a short film featuring your vision of what sharing that special place with someone special might look like. Insert this short film in your profile after you mention your favorite destination.

Write a Screenplay

My favorite city is Paris, and I wrote my screenplay to appeal to a specific type of woman who shares my passion. My film begins with my lover and me strolling arm in arm along the tree-shaded Left Bank of the Seine River, on a warm, sunny morning, stopping at the vendor stalls along the way to the Muse` D'Orsay, the old train station converted into an Impressionist museum. We spend a few hours gazing at magnificent art, whispering in each other's ears, enjoying the romantic quality of Renoir, Degas, Monet, and other brilliant Impressionist painters. Afterward, we share a late afternoon lunch at a sidewalk café. Then we walk back to our hotel and make love until we fall asleep in each other's arms. When we wake up, we go out for cocktails at the historic Les Deus Magot bar, and after enjoying its visual treats, share a romantic dinner in a candle-lit, neighborhood restaurant.

Whether or not Paris is your favorite destination is unimportant. What is important is that my Paris fantasy film worked. It received a large number of enthusiastic responses from women who shared my vision and my passion. Most importantly, my film was romantic, but also realistic. The best possible result was that my sweetheart was one of the women who responded to my film, and she was exactly the woman I'd hoped to attract.

If you write your screenplay for a specific man or woman, you'll be deluged with emails from the people you hoped to attract. Whether your favorite place is Paris or camping under the stars, focus your short film on a very specific audience of like-minded men or women. No one's film will appeal to everyone, but that's okay, because it's not the quantity of responses that matter, it's the quality. You can attract an army of frogs with boring, generic information, but your profile is a terrific opportunity to reach single boomers that share your particular enthusiasms. Write your profile as if your dating success depends on its quality, because it does.

Write With Passion

Whatever your personal interests, it's the manner in which you share them that will make your profile appealing. Skip the trite walks on the beach, wine by the fireplace, and romantic, candlelit dinners, when given the opportunity to write what is most real and relevant to you. Focus on those passions you'd enjoy sharing with a partner. Remember that every passion you write about should be described in terms of sharing it. You're looking for a date, and hopefully someone to share your life with, not showing off.

Are you an avid bicyclist, jogger, hiker, cook, singer, motorcyclist, dancer, mountain or rock climber, spiritual seeker, poet, exercise enthusiast, yoga practitioner, writer, live music lover, videographer, theatergoer, independent film enthusiast, wine connoisseur, musician, or passionate about any of a myriad of possible interests? Don't be afraid of appearing too over the top about your favorite activities, because lukewarm isn't nearly as attractive as passionate to the right person, and that man or woman the only person you're trying to appeal to. Think of dating in terms of an a la carte menu, not an all you can eat buffet.

Aim for the specific person you feel would enjoy sharing your passion with. Perhaps you're an amateur theater performer who would like to share his or her acting passion with another enthusiastic fledgling actor or actress. Have you been in a bicycle or foot race, written something special, have a performance art talent to share, or is there a special gourmet dinner you only cook with or for someone special? The point is to intrigue a stranger enough to cause them to respond to you, another stranger.

Boring, incomplete, or lazily written profiles are quickly scanned and quickly forgotten. Sure, in a perfect world everyone would be willing to read between the lines to glean what a terrific person you are, but the dating world isn't nearly perfect. You're going to have to create success with ingenuity and energy. Halfway measures won't entice the man or woman you want to meet, because your ideal date won't respond to a minimum effort.

Younger Isn't Always Better

This is a sensitive topic, and one that drives boomer women over the edge. It's worth mentioning, since it's one of the major complaints boomer women lodge against boomer men. I devoted an entire chapter to boomer women and their virtues, as well as a chapter on boomer men. Both are likely in the prime of their adult lives, emotionally and physically.

I urge boomer men not to fall into the trap of dating younger women as a panacea for a midlife crisis, dating blues, or a painful divorce, because it's a Band- aid at best. It's important to get a firm grip on how you're feeling about yourself before you date, because whatever it takes for you to feel better after a bitter breakup is your work, and it can't be outsourced to someone because she's younger and less worldly. Besides, do you really want to explain that Paul McCartney wasn't always a solo act, or that Yoko Ono isn't Michelle Obama's gown designer? Boomer women are attractive partners in so many vital ways, and since none of us looks the same as we once did, there are many other far more important considerations. Just because your boomer ex-wife or girlfriend may have been an angry, bitter woman, doesn't mean that all boomer women are angry and bitter. There's great comfort in a relationship with a woman who has shared your experiences, and with whom you can relate easily. Boomer women have a lot of love to give, and what they ask in return is emotional warmth, respect, and commitment. It seems a fair bargain.

Choosing a life partner is a serious decision, and it should involve more than a young body, or a false sense of superiority and virility an older man may feel that's due at least in part to being more worldly and powerful, because he has lived longer than his young date, and knows more about life. A relationship is about an authentic partnership, not a training program for inexperienced women. Younger women are terrific, and my intention isn't to disparage them. To evolved boomer men, they're like a cake that's not fully baked. Picking a boomer woman is right for lots of reasons, not the least of which is that they understand the significance and value of friendship as a major aspect of a relationship. If you're planning to spend the rest of your life with someone, emotional intimacy and friendship have to be a part of it to succeed. While the term "cougar" comes to mind when I read women's profiles that insist that only men twenty to thirty years younger need apply, this isn't typical for boomer women, most of whom are looking for men close to their age. It makes good sense to mention your interest in finding a partner within five years or so of your age unless you insist on younger men or women.

Typecasting Your Dates

We all have character actors we love in their typecast roles. James Gandolfini was my all-time favorite gangster, because he brought an amazing range of emotion to his character. His face could show joy, anger, sadness, and wild-eyed craziness, simultaneously. Mr.

Gandolfini played other roles well, but he'll always be Tony Soprano to me, and to millions who waited impatiently for each new episode of _The Sopranos_.

Boomers frequently typecast dates, and the longer we date the narrower our parameters may become. There's a big difference between being focused and being narrow-minded. Notice the non-negotiable terms in the personal ads that boomers write to describe their only acceptable dates. Their preferences are frequently mentioned in absolute terms, some stating they don't want responses from anyone that doesn't meet the casting call perfectly. Tall, medium height, big-breasts, small breasts, dark hair, blond, shaved head, muscular, thin, chubby, in shape, blue eyes, handsome, beautiful, athletic, hiker, biker, drinker, non-drinker, religious, atheist, spiritual, and a myriad of other terms used to describe the only type of man or woman they're willing to consider. We become so stuck in our typecast fantasies that we become blind to any other possibilities, so much so that we automatically look past anyone who doesn't fit our typecast fantasy to a T.

The strangest aspect of boomer typecasting is that it doesn't seem to matter that it hasn't ever worked. We continue typecasting our dates by convincing ourselves that we're choosing the right type, but just the wrong people within our type. Our narrow parameters eliminate a treasure trove of possibilities, but we stubbornly remain stuck on in a circular path leading nowhere.

I had a friend in his late forties who was marrying for the fourth time. Like his three previous wives, the fourth was short, blonde, and had large breasts, and like his third wife who I'd known, number four was mean-spirited and sarcastic, particularly in public. When I asked why he was marrying such a hard woman, he replied, "I don't love her like I did the others so if we break up I won't get my heart broken again." I'd never heard anyone embrace such a negative rationale for marrying. He was stuck in his typecast and couldn't see beyond it, to his detriment.

After dating online for a while without great success, I decided to take a closer look at my choices to see if I might notice a pattern. It was immediately and abundantly clear I had a type I'd chosen, nearly exclusively. Even though this type had never worked for me, I held onto my flawed fantasy with stubborn determination. I was going to make that square peg fit into that round hole no matter how much I had to whittle that peg.

It was only after I let go of my typecast fantasy that I met my partner, who embodies every quality I'd hoped to find in a woman. That she wasn't my historical physical type, but was perfect nonetheless, was a wake-up call. Sarah is tall, thin, has a prominent nose, and brown curly hair, not at all a match with my previous type, which was short, fuller-figured, ski jump nose, and straight blonde hair. The floodgates opened when I let go of my fantasy type, and Sarah rode in on the rushing wave. All that was necessary was a willingness to look past my type. In truth, I wasn't eager to try this, but since my type had never worked, I felt a new paradigm was worth considering.

Interestingly, Sarah also had a failed, physical fantasy type, and I wasn't that guy. She was just as surprised as I was about the results of letting go of our types. We both recognized that our core values and beliefs were the same, and that we shared the same passions in life. We're enjoying the best relationship either of us can remember. We laugh and play like best friends. We're also having the best sex imaginable.

Sarah's beauty struck me like a lightning bolt when we first met, and I was instantly grateful I'd decided to think outside of my typecast box and contact her. While Sarah is the most beautiful woman I've been in relationship with, more importantly, she has every quality, core value, belief, and characteristic I desired. I'm not the smartest guy on the planet, but I'm smart enough to finally learn the typecast lesson. Besides, isn't repeating the same behavior, and hoping for a different result, the classic definition of insanity?

If you think outside of your fantasy typecast box you might discover you've actually grown beyond it anyway. How can you tell if you're open to a new type? It's as simple as looking at the next man or woman you meet with what the Buddhists call beginner's eyes. This means seeing the next man or woman as if they are the first man or woman you've ever seen, instead of immediately comparing that person to your failed type. Think about your past relationships, and you'll probably notice you've typecast most, if not all your dating choices. All that's required to open up new possibilities is to remove the blinders that keep you on a circular path. It's worth considering.

You Don't Need a Geography Lesson

Geography should also be given consideration when choosing dates. While the notion that love can overcome anything may be true, why put yourself through an unnecessarily difficult exercise? Unless you live in a sparsely populated area, date close to your zip code to make spending time with your new love interest easy. I live in the densely populated Bay Area, so I'm puzzled why singles living here would consider a long distance relationship. I dated a woman who lived an hour away, and more in traffic. Sitting in bumper-to-bumper traffic got really old, really fast. The fatigue factor wasn't the only reason we stopped dating, but it was a factor. Sarah and I live fifteen minutes from each other, which means we spend our time together, instead of in our cars. Relationships are difficult enough under the best circumstances, so make dating easier by minimizing the driving time. If you're thinking about getting into a relationship that requires an airline ticket, think again. Come on folks, haven't we all been through enough pain and suffering? Is it really possible that the only appropriate person for you requires a plane ticket? Dating smart includes dating as locally as possible.

Know Who You Are

The first task I assign my date coaching clients, before they even post a profile, or go online to look at other people's profiles, is to make a list of the five or six best characteristics they feel describe them most accurately and that they feel proud and special about. While some clients find this exercise difficult, knowing who you are is the first step toward finding a suitable partner.

This list is actually your list, in terms of describing you as well as the person you hope to meet, because you want to meet someone as much like you as possible. Making a list worked so well for me, and for thousands who have written me, that I consider it an essential dating tool. Your short list should include what you feel are your most sterling qualities and characteristics.

If you find it difficult to make your list, consider that you've been through a lot of changes over the years, and perhaps you might want to reconsider the qualities and characteristics that best describe you today. Since you'll be using your list as a guide for choosing potential online dates, start with your core values and beliefs, because they shouldn't ever be compromised.

What qualities and characteristics best describe you? Does your list include integrity, emotional intelligence, sensitivity, physical fitness, spiritual or religious attitudes, and any others you feel make up the authentic you?

When reading a potential date's online profile, pay attention to whether or not they share your qualities, characteristics, and core values and beliefs. Please don't underestimate their significance or overlook glaring differences. Avoid the trap that differences can be worked out with someone you haven't met, because even if you find someone who's a perfect match, there will still be issues and differences to work out. If you have similar personality types and coping skills, you won't have to begin from zero and struggle each time an issue arises, as you might with someone who doesn't share your qualities and characteristics.

Doppelganger Fear

Not surprisingly some boomer men and women reject the notion of pairing with their twin, and fear is typically their reason. Whatever a boomer's worst characteristics, some fear their twin will share all their negative qualities as well as their positive ones. This isn't necessarily true but, even if it were, sharing similar issues offers both people an opportunity to work through those issues together.

The Good News

Most importantly, your twin will share your temperament, tastes, life philosophy, motivation, sexuality, and core values and beliefs. No one should ever consider these negotiable, particularly core values and beliefs, so finding a partner who embodies them is well worth the search. Granted even your twin may not work out in a relationship, because there are other factors that take time to develop and notice, but at a minimum, you're at the starting gate together.

Successful relationships create time to discuss the problems that partners bump up against that are causing friction. A couple that shares the same characteristics and personalities is more likely to readily resolve problems. If they're opposites, their relationship will often be engulfed in flames, because the differences in characteristics and personality types will become insurmountable stumbling blocks that will ultimately result in one, or both partners, to hoist a white flag out of frustration.

A devoutly religious person won't feel at ease with an atheist for long, and a type A personality will overwhelm a more relaxed one. A physical fitness enthusiast isn't going to resonate with a couch potato. Someone who has well developed emotional skills, and expresses his or her feelings easily, will become frustrated with someone who doesn't or can't. Being selective should never be construed as being too picky. Being selective works, because it addresses specific, non-negotiable qualities. The date you choose reflects your sense of self-esteem, and if you're picking dates that don't match your qualities and characteristics, consider the reasons. You deserve the best partner on the planet.

Date Safely

Online dating safety is a major concern. Few, if any, of the senior dating websites perform more than minimal vetting for membership. Online dating sites have unwittingly opened their doors to cheaters, scammers, liars, and worse. It's incumbent upon website users to do their own due diligence to protect themselves.

There are a few simple guidelines to follow that can help keep you safe, and while most are aimed at women, men are also at risk. A woman should never give her telephone number to a man first. He should give his, and if he seems reluctant, hang up and be grateful, because he likely had questionable motives for being secretive. Never invite someone into your home who you just began dating. Wait until you feel you know them reasonably well, and even then you might want to invite friends to join you. I invited a woman to dinner too early after meeting her, and after she drank the better part of a bottle of wine, she refused to leave, insisting she lived there too. I had to call my neighbor and ask her to help me remove my date. It was ugly. Lesson learned.

When the coffee date is over, leave alone. Anyone who refuses to meet you for coffee on a first date, during the day, is another bullet you likely dodged.

Never allow money to enter into a new relationship. A man or woman who asks for money, no matter the circumstances, is not someone you want to get to know better. An email from another country automatically gets deleted, and emails from other states fall into the same category, unless you're looking for a pen pal. Never assume your dating website is looking out for your safety.

While I haven't been a member of every boomer dating website, I've belonged to several, such as Match.com, Seniors Meet, Plenty of Fish, HowAboutWe, and OKCupid, to name a few. Most offer a fair amount of space to write your profile. I met my sweetheart on OKCupid, which offered a large number of potential dates in my area, and was free. Most websites have introductory offers, and some are free, while others offer a free month. Avoid the low prices offered for extended memberships, and wait until you're sure which you want to remain with.

Other Venues

Online dating offers boomers a terrific opportunity to meet each other, and I'm not aware of any venue having as many potential dates. But there are other places where single boomers can meet. There are local clubs in most communities for bicycling, jogging, hiking, sailing, books, amateur theater, wine tasting, dinner groups, and other interests, and many have senior contingents.

Community volunteering is another possibility, and if you choose something that appeals to you, you already know that a man or woman you meet in that volunteer activity shares your interest.

None of these activities affords you the opportunity to prescreen members in the depth that online dating does. The anonymity of online dating takes some of the sting out of choosing a stranger to begin a dialogue.

Take a break from online dating when you become fatigued or frustrated. I knew it was time to walk away for a while when opening my emails, or writing them, felt like a burden. A week offline can renew your spirits and put you in a better dating mood.

Remember, the perfect partner you're looking for, is also looking for you. Your worlds just have to collide to meet, and online dating offers the greatest opportunity for that to happen.

Chapter Seven:
From Online to the First Date

The reality of boomer dating is that most boomers will go on a great number of first dates before they finally meet someone they feel is special. What makes this even more of a painstaking process is that many boomers don't have the skillset to understand when a second date is appropriate. While it's not a tragedy to go on a second date, even after not feeling there was much potential on the first, boomers don't have a lot of time to waste. The huge number of potential dates online is staggering—and the fun of sampling that lengthy list can wear thin fast. Even if your first dates are as short as meeting for coffee, they still take time and energy—and they can quickly become an emotional drain.

Who Are You?

Throwing figurative darts at online profiles, and hoping for positive results, is naive and extremely unlikely to yield a life partner. Boomers need to do better than choosing dates randomly if they hope to find the special person they're looking for. To insure you don't waste time or energy dating inappropriate men or women, you first have to keep in mind what makes you special, which means understanding yourself on a deeper level. As I mentioned, your list of personal qualities and characteristics should match the person you want to date nearly exactly if you hope to find a life partner. It may take some extended reflection, but you'll be flying blind, and hoping not to crash, without considering character.

What's the Point?

The point of making a list of your best characteristics was to help you find a partner who shares all or nearly all of those characteristics on your list. I urge readers not to fall into that black hole that is opposites attract. I'll personalize this to make the process easier to follow. I'm a type A personality and I can still remember a relationship I was in with a woman years ago, who was a type B. When we reached the point where I was finishing her sentences for her out of frustration and impatience, I realized we were a mismatch. We were opposites, and even though I appreciated her low-key demeanor, and she liked my high energy, after a while our differences caused unresolvable friction.

Someone who matches your physical and emotional energy levels as close to perfectly as possible is a solid match. There's more to consider of course, but at least you'll be on the same page, in terms of who you both are. While I do know a couple in a successful relationship that has very different personality types, they're a rare pair in my experience. Choosing a perfect match, in terms of characteristics, will take a lot of the sting out of finding appropriate people to date.

Dating Isn't a Numbers Game

If only a small percentage of men or women are able to answer the six questions in this chapter on a first date, in addition to any other questions you feel are important, that's all right because you want to swim in a small pool with the best potential candidates. Popular wisdom notwithstanding, dating is not a numbers game and kissing lots of frogs is neither necessary, nor the point. The fastest road leading to dating burnout is indiscriminate online dating.

6 Questions to Ask Your Date

There are six questions you should ask your first date that will help determine the viability of a second. These questions cut right to the chase, and there's no wiggle room regarding the appropriate responses. The answers will narrow the field considerably, but that's the point. Good looks, money, social status, and other less important qualities don't make up for inappropriate answers. Your future relationship happiness depends in great part on the person you choose as a partner, and these questions are intended to reach people on a deeper level than the typical questions daters typically ask. What's your sign, what's your all-time favorite movie, and do you like sushi, don't matter a whit in terms of making good choices.

There's no prize for making the most bad, second date choices, and while these questions aren't the only important ones to ask, they can tell you in a few minutes, what might otherwise take months to determine if you don't ask them. The concern most women frequently mention about asking these questions is their fear that their date will react badly to them. That has never happened to me, or any of my clients, and none of my readers has reported this occurring either. Facing your fears, and asking your date relevant questions, will seem more than just a worthwhile exercise if you dodge a bullet because you asked them. While it's impractical to think your date will be totally transparent about who they are, and what makes them tick, on a first date, that doesn't mean he or she should be shut down either.

I used this list of questions when I met my partner, and she answered each of the six questions easily and gladly. My clients, and thousands of readers, have also used similar questions with success. Women frequently write to tell me that there aren't any men who can answer these questions appropriately, but after working with men in small groups for twenty-five years, I disagree. Men may take a while and answer them carefully, but that isn't a negative. Since it's meant to narrow the field quickly and accurately, the washout rate will naturally be high. That's okay because you're looking for a life partner, not just a date.

But be prepared to have these questions turned around on you. That's only fair. Sometimes it can feel awkward to just run down a list of questions with a date. A better methodology is to bring up the issues suggested in these questions by talking about yourself, which means answering the questions before you pose them to your date.

Prescreen Your Dates

You may want to ask the first of the six questions by mentioning your own personal growth path, and this issue may come up before you meet in person. We're boomers, and we've been around long enough to realize that our lives work better if we did some amount of self-examination. Talking about any work you've done will encourage a potential date to talk about theirs. This doesn't have to include psychotherapy. A good response might be a book you or your potential date read about personal growth.

Problem resolution skills aren't innate, and every relationship will run into troublesome issues. The difference between staying together and deepening the emotional connection, or breaking up, may depend on a couple's ability to work together to resolve conflict. It would be cynical to help boomers date and meet someone, and not offer a heads up regarding what's going to be required to keep a relationship healthy. A poor response to this question may not be a deal killer, but the answer reflects a potential date's interest in getting on top of the types of issues that require skills to resolve.

So be brave and begin a dialogue about emotional health. It's a conversation you'll have when problems come up, so there's no point in delaying the inevitable. Don't get stuck on this question, because if a potential date has little or no interest in being the best, potential partner possible, that's worth knowing up front.

The 6 Questions

1. Have you ever been in individual or group therapy, been in a men's or women's group, attended a relationship or personal growth workshop, a relationship lecture or workshop, read any books, magazine or newspaper articles about personal growth or relationships, or participated in

any type of activity that reflects an interest in becoming a better man or woman, and relationship partner?

This first question points directly to a person's potential relationship skills. Since relationships invariably face problems, a man or woman who hasn't shown any interest in emotional consciousness is unlikely to have the skills required to work problems out to a good conclusion. Boomers have lived through the longest period of self-help and self-improvement ever, and someone who has ignored what was hard to ignore, is a questionable candidate. Most boomers realize that personal growth is an ongoing process.

The problem resolution skills required to keep a relationship on track are not second nature to many people. This is learned behavior, and it necessitates some amount of effort. A boomer who has ignored their emotional issues and chosen not to get on top of them, will struggle to feel their own pain and will unlikely be able to feel yours either. Since successful relationships typically involve two emotionally savvy and capable partners, a lack of developed emotional coping skills is not a good start.

I urged a client to ask this first question to a fellow she met online. He told her that no one had ever asked him this question before, and his answer was that his life experiences were his personal growth path. While I believe he learned a lot from his life experiences, little of what he learned relates to developing emotional skills. I stress this point because one person who has done inner work can't carry the emotional weight for two in a relationship. When arguments become circular, which means they never get resolved, it's usually because one or both partners lack the skills to share how they're feeling, and revert instead to what they think about each other.

If a man or woman can't share how they're feeling when conflict arises, the result is often making angry statements about the other person, which generates the same in return. That circular argument won't ever get resolved, and the issue is sure to continue popping up because it wasn't. In addition to these skills, both partners have to be willing to admit when their behavior is the cause of the problem. In truth, it can be difficult to work out issues even when both partners are skilled in this arena, but when the dust settles and the anger subsides, it's their learned behavior that helps create resolution.

A boomer who has avoided all the aforementioned is unlikely to have the problem resolution skills relationships require, since he or she hasn't faced their demons yet. With rare exception, every boomer has had issues they needed to work through. It's not that every boomer is unhinged, but rather that every boomer has faced challenges and circumstances that left them emotionally scarred to some extent. If someone has glibly ignored these issues, then by default, those issues automatically become the other person's burden. And carrying someone else's emotional baggage gets really old, really fast. One partner can't single-handedly create intimacy and trust in a relationship. A successful relationship requires two stewards, both of whom have at least minimal emotional skills.

2. Do you have a job or some other means of supporting yourself?

Becoming someone's financial life support system is unlikely to get your relationship off to a propitious start. Think about what carrying a partner financially would mean – and what you would expect in return. In the many relationships I've observed, in which one person supports the other, there are nearly always expectations connected with that support, whether spoken or not. Financially lopsided relationships frequently get bogged down in control issues, with the money partner wielding the most control. These arrangements can get ugly, and resentments build on both sides until they become untenable. Equality in every aspect of a relationship, including financial, is critical. This is not a good basis for building intimacy and trust, and the relationship usually ends with the supported person's bags at the curb. The exception to this is a marriage in which one person stays at home and takes care of the family business. But this is a dating book and what works in marriages doesn't necessarily work in fledgling relationships. There's no free lunch. Unless you're planning to finance the entire relationship, which rarely works well since it gives one partner power over the other, this is critical.

3. What core values and beliefs guide you?

Shared basic values and beliefs are essential for the long-term success of a relationship. If your boomer date doesn't have or can't articulate his or her philosophy for living life in a positive, meaningful manner, you won't be able to fill that void. Since your core values and beliefs are non-negotiable, a date who can't articulate his or hers is a non-starter. What I've heard from people who ignore these differences is that in the long-term, the relationship becomes contentious and disappointing. Your twin shares your core values and beliefs.

4. What did you learn from your last relationship?

This is an especially important question, and anyone who answers, "Nothing," should cause you concern, because they're either unconscious or arrogant. It's rare when one person single-handedly wrecks a relationship; it takes two people to make a relationship succeed or fail. A response of "Nothing" may be a sign that your date doesn't take personal responsibility for his or her behavior, which makes that person a terrible choice for a partner. This question points to a person's sense of personal accountability, which leads to an all too common thread frequently mentioned by both men and women. A boomer who hasn't learned that it's okay to admit fault, and is willing to learn from his or her failures, will tend to blame you for all the problems that arise, which makes any possible resolution dependent on your absorbing the blame. You deserve a partner who is emotionally open, willing to be vulnerable, and who understands that admitting mistakes is a sign of strength, not weakness. Apologizing is another stubborn issue that some men and women find challenging. I urge everyone to bite the bullet and admit when you're wrong.

5.   Do you have any same sex friends?

A man or woman who lacks same sex friends likely has trust issues, which is why that person is a loner in the first place; he or she may pose a relationship risk, and unless you want to be that person's entire social universe, a heavy burden, it may be best to move on. It's critical that both partners have a life outside of the relationship, and that includes friendships. Much of what men and women know about trust and relationships is learned through their friendships. A woman I dated briefly told me that she didn't have time for friends. I ignored this red flag, but regretted it when I realized she had serious trust issues that she'd never come to grips with. As my mentor frequently opined about relationships, "Where there's no trust, there's no love." Boomers have been around long enough to work through their issues, at least to the extent that they can establish friendships. Since friendship is a major component of all the best relationships, someone unable or unwilling to make friends is unlikely to become yours either.

6.   What's your sense of humor like? What do you find funny?

Every relationship gets into trouble occasionally, and a sense of humor, especially about oneself, can make the difference between working issues out easily, or not at all. If your date's sense of humor matches yours, you'll have lots of entertainment options to share. Don't ignore this unless you don't have a sense of humor, or you're prepared to laugh alone.

There Is a Plethora of Good Men

I received an email from a woman who had read a partial list of these questions in an article I wrote, and she commented that my list made her laugh because not one of the men she'd met on a date could answer any of these questions satisfactorily. She further doubted any man could. Her comment was her truth, in terms of her experience, but it seemed wrongheaded to me, because assuming she was able to answer these questions satisfactorily, the notion that there aren't *any* men that also could seemed short-sighted. You get what you aim for in every aspect of life, including dating, and if you aim low, you shouldn't be surprised your dates aren't productive. "All the good men are taken," simply isn't true and that attitude is more reflective of making bad choices.

Since poor choices never yield positive results, a dismal batting average with men doesn't mean there's something wrong or missing in the entire boomer male population. Many boomer men and women have faced their issues, and have done some amount of personal growth work to help overcome them. If you decide to date a boomer, man or woman, who hasn't been introspective or done any personal growth work, and you think a good outcome is still likely, think again. There aren't any successful relationships that never require the skills that personal growth work teaches people. If both partners eschewed this type of inner work, failure is all but guaranteed. Virtually no one is born with well-developed interpersonal skills. It takes a concerted effort to learn these skills. Developing good self-esteem is part of this work.

What Else?

What else is appropriate or inappropriate to talk about? If you want to talk about sex I suggest you make it a general conversation and not about you and your potential partner having sex together. That kind of sexual push is a turnoff to most, if not all, women and quite a few men too. Sex is a conversation to be eased into when the moment is right. Besides asking the six questions it's helpful to keep the conversation light, since you don't know each other and personalizing your sexual desire about someone you don't know isn't light.

Smart Dating

Asking these questions is an aspect of smart dating, and if you get promising answers to all of them, feel free to ask any others you think are important. Please don't minimize or ignore inappropriate answers, because you'll pay the price for doing so, soon enough. Finding the right partner in your boomer years isn't a needle in a haystack or a numbers game, and no less than a perfect score will do. If you can answer these questions with appropriate answers, you have every right to expect that a candidate for the position of your life partner can answer them equally well. If you ask these questions and listen to the answers with a discriminating ear, you should know whether or not your date has the potential to be your life partner before you finish your coffee.

It's Supposed To Be Fun Too

Remember to have fun. I realize asking a first date serious questions can feel like the opposite of fun, so I'm not suggesting you sit down and rattle off six questions. Work them into the conversation. Talking about your friends is an easy way to ask about whether or not your date has friends. Mentioning some type of inner work you've done, paves the way for your date to jump into the conversation and talk about his or her path. If you talk about your ex-wife or girlfriend in a non-judgmental manner, and emphasize what you learned from that failed relationship, your date should feel safe talking about his or her relationship failures.

Parting Isn't Always Easy

It takes a kind heart and emotional honesty to end a date well, which means respecting both your date and yourself. Sure, there's some awkwardness associated with ending a coffee date that didn't go anywhere, but you're not responsible for the date's lack of success. Men in particular tend to end coffee dates with, "I'll call you," even when they know in their hearts that they won't. I found thanking a woman for meeting me, and telling her I'm not feeling any relationship potential, very difficult. Ultimately I learned to be emotionally honest at the end of a first date. It spared my date's feelings, and I felt better about handling a difficult task well.

Roller Coaster Rides

We've all been on relationship roller coaster rides, and some of us have been on far too many, so being circumspect when choosing appropriate dates should become your new normal. If you think back on your failed relationships, it shouldn't be hard to identify what the issues were with him or her that caused you to break up. My guess is that your ex wouldn't have been able to answer the six questions, or even some of them appropriately. Okay, you didn't have the six questions or your list then, but you do now, so date smart.

Finicky is Good

Is being picky part of smart dating? Yes, it absolutely is, and it's a critical part of smart dating. Unless your ultimate goal is to simply continue dating, you have to be willing to be picky. Dating with the purpose of finding your life partner, doesn't mean choosing someone who belongs in the category of second best. Treat yourself with the same respect you would a friend, and be your own best friend when choosing dates.

Chapter Eight:
The First Date

A Plague of Frogs

A first date for a boomer can be an unnerving experience, because it's frequently a double-edged sword. Sure, there's lots of excitement, and maybe even some sweet fantasies attached to meeting someone new, because there's always the possibility they might have partner potential. The other side of that coin is the sense of dread that seasoned dating boomers feel anticipating one more, in a long line of disappointing first dates. Your prior first date experiences have convinced you that you're going to have to kiss a lot more frogs before you meet someone special, but even smooching a bunch of amphibians doesn't guarantee your life partner will be one of them. The number of frogs you end up dating before you meet your life partner depends to a great extent on how you date; smart dating can limit your exposure to frogs.

**A Frog Disclaimer

Frogs come in all shapes, sizes, and colors. It's not a date's physical qualities that determine if he or she is a frog, because physical types vary widely. If you've been labeled a frog, it's likely related to your behavior. I've heard enough comments from women that indicate a man's physicality wasn't the criteria for designating him a frog. Tall, handsome, in-shape, and a full head of hair, aren't nearly enough to be frog proof. For some reason, I rarely hear men use the word frog to describe a bad date. What makes a date earn that unenviable tag?

Looking Like a Frog Is Self-Defeating

Since it's nearly always behavior that designates a frog, I would have thought every boomer guy understood the importance of his attitude, in terms of making a positive first date impression. I was surprised when a several women shared similar first date stories with me about men who showed up at their doors looking slovenly and unkempt. After repeatedly hearing variations on this theme, I realized that some men are still in the dark about the importance of showing up for a first date looking their best. An unkempt appearance reflects a less than casual attitude that women find insulting. Women generally take as much time as is necessary to look, at the very least, well groomed.

The number of women that have commented to me about first dates who appeared at their door wearing old shorts, T-shirts that barely covered their bellies, and flip flops, became too numerous to ignore, so some amount of dialogue on this topic seems appropriate. "This is who I am, take it or leave it," is neither an effective, nor a well-mannered first date strategy. Laziness isn't a virtue, and neither is sloppiness; everyone needs to make a concerted effort to look as presentable as possible on a first date. There are no excuses for looking like you just walked off the beach. While this is basic and obvious to the vast majority of men, a sufficient number of women's stories suggest it's not universally true.

I dated on and off between relationships for decades, and I can't recall one woman that didn't show up to a first date looking attractive, which had nothing to do with her beauty, and everything to do with the effort she made about her appearance.

Guys, you don't have to be a clotheshorse or a male fashion model to look attractive. It's as simple as tucking your clean, pressed shirt into your clean jeans or khakis, polishing your shoes, and combing your hair. Whatever physical shape you're in, you can improve your image substantially simply by dressing as if you're going out to dinner with friends. Informal is fine, and jeans and a sport shirt are okay for nearly all activities, as long as they're clean and neat.

Shaving is a reasonable effort to make, current male fashion models notwithstanding, if you hope to impress a woman, unless you're sporting a beard or mustache. Just imagine how you'd feel if your date showed up looking like she dressed herself out of her dirty laundry basket, after working out at the gym. You're not making a statement when you show up looking like you don't care. You're making a mistake.

Some women have suggested that the reason a fair number of men act as if they're doing women a favor asking them out, is that women greatly outnumber men on most online dating sites, and their unkempt appearance simply reflects a perceived advantage. C'mon guys, that's juvenile and foolish. Boomer women have earned our respect, and you're not going to impress any woman by showing up looking like you don't care. Good personal grooming and hygiene are the minimum effort, and I suggest making a more concerted one.

All Frogs Aren't Male

Now that slovenly male frogs have been chastised, it's only fair to mention that women are also sometimes frogs, although rarely for their personal hygiene or wardrobe. Only a very tiny percentage of boomer women would feel it's appropriate to show up for a first date looking unkempt.

What constitutes a female frog may be open to debate, but there's one issue in particular that a large number of men have suggested qualifies as frog behavior.

A boomer woman who expects to be wined and dined by a man on a first date and/or every date thereafter, is pretty much a universal turnoff to most men, and merits a frog nomination. The notion that women have achieved equality, and that men are still on the hook to pay for everything, can turn a woman into a frog instantly.

A *buy me, give me, show me, take me* attitude, that some women convey is disturbing to lots of men, and insulting as well. It's not necessarily just about the money either. It's the attitude that's offensive.

Women fought hard to gain equal footing in every aspect of life, and while some room for fairer treatment is still warranted, few boomer guys want to be taken for granted, particularly around being expected to pay for every date or dinner out. There are as many boomer women with as much or more money than their boomer men dates, so it seems unreasonable to invoke fair treatment and equality for women on one hand, and suggest it's a man's responsibility to pay for everything on the other.

While a woman who avoids looking at the check when the waiter brings it is sending a message that she expects her date to pay, there are an increasing number of women who reach into their purses when the check arrives. Times are changing, and the number of women who expect to always be treated is dwindling. Even if a man has money to burn, that doesn't change the gender paradigm. Equal means being treated the same, financially, and a woman's offer to share the bill is viewed as fair and considerate by most men. It's also appreciated, and a man can decline her offer if he chooses.

A number of women have written stating that they agree with the premise that fair is fair, as regards paying their way on dates, and some have mentioned that they intentionally suggest restaurants for dates where they know they can afford to pay their share of the bill. I remember when the check came after the first dinner out with my partner. She reached into her purse and suggested we split the bill. I appreciated her gesture, but said I'd take care of this one, and that she could get the next one. We've been doing this for nearly two years and we both feel good about this arrangement since we're partners in every sense.

A Door Isn't a Sexual Barrier

A woman wrote me about a situation that immediately turned her first date into a frog. He picked her up at her home, and when they got to his car he said, "Since you're equal now, you can open your own door." Ouch! C'mon fella, really? I consider opening doors for a woman, whether a car, a restaurant, or any door for that matter, to be a gentlemanly, gracious thing to do, which has nothing to do with equal, and everything to do with being courteous and respectful. Her date's comment was meant to insult, not congratulate. The rest of her date didn't get any better, which didn't surprise her since it began with a figurative slap in the face.

Sex and Respect

Most boomer women label a guy a frog if he becomes aggressive about demanding first date sex. What part of "I don't have sex on a first date," don't you get? Trying to convince a boomer woman with good self-esteem, that she should sexually satisfy a virtual stranger, qualifies a guy for the frog hall of shame. Respect between boomers is fundamental, including sex, which for most boomer women is inexorably linked with emotional intimacy. If you're a single guy recently out of a long-term relationship, this is valuable information. If you routinely attempt to engage boomer women in casual sex on first dates, you're a slow learner.

Angry Frogs

A man or a woman, who spends a first date disparaging his or her ex-husband, ex-wife, ex-boyfriend, or ex-girlfriend, qualifies for a frog collar for wasting someone's time, by using them as a sounding board for their unresolved anger.

Being Able To Trust Is Basic

A man or woman with a chip on their shoulder about not trusting the opposite sex, because they were betrayed in the past, qualifies as a wounded frog, which is worse than a regular frog, because there's no quick fix. To intimate that trust is still a major issue because of the manner in which someone was treated in the past, is a red flag. Being present and in the moment with a first date is not only courteous, it's only fair. No one wants to feel held responsible for how someone else treated their date in the past, and no one smart is going to be willing to fight the uphill battle that means breaking through someone's protective walls to reach that person's heart either. If you haven't healed from your last relationship, for heaven's sake, stay home until you do, otherwise you'll be tagged as a frog.

Boomers Remember When Manners Were Normal

Suffice to say, men and women are equally capable of behaving like frogs. Behaving like a prig is inexcusable, especially since both parties had to agree to the date. Dating manners seem to have gone missing, particularly since online dating began, since quite a few people believe that anonymity makes it acceptable to be rude. Most boomers likely remember growing up in a time when being polite and respectful was considered normal. I've had a few dates from hell, and I've felt misled by women at times, but I didn't resort to frog behavior, although I admit it wasn't always easy. If a date turns out badly, or you feel disappointed, simply say thanks and walk away with your dignity intact. That type of behavior would go a long way toward limiting frog spottings.

Why A Wish List Works

I've written several articles for *The Huffington Post, About.com*, and *AARP* about why it's critical to date using a list. In my experience, and the experiences of thousands of men and women that have commented on my articles, a wish list of some sort is a requirement. Consider not being given a menu at a restaurant and hoping you'll enjoy whatever the waiter decides to bring you for dinner. That's a gamble not many people would feel comfortable taking, for obvious reasons. Dating without a wish list is similarly shooting in the dark and hoping for the best.

The reason for creating a list of criteria is the same as the reason you read a restaurant menu, i.e., not every boomer's online profile is going to fill you with hope and excitement. You need to choose with at least the same level of personal taste and discrimination you would ordering dinner at a restaurant.

The colossal number of single women overwhelmed me when I initially started dating online, and I made the rooky mistake of contacting lots of women at random, mostly based on photos. I went on countless coffee dates with women, none of who were remotely what I was looking for. I eventually figured out why my approach wasn't working, and in addition to creating the list of six questions, I made another list of interests that I felt passionate about, and wanted to share with a woman. Be thoughtful when deciding on these activities, because you're defining your future partner.

In Addition

I'm an avid hiker, so a physically active woman was high on my list. I also had a short list of interests I wanted to share that included the arts, museums and galleries, music, and the ballet. Other activities I listed were cooking, motorcycling, and anything to do with the ocean or beach, which I wanted to share with a like-minded woman. I'm a strong advocate for social justice and the political causes that reflect that sentiment, and I wanted to meet a woman with similar political/philosophical leanings. I also wanted a travel companion for adventure and fun. I've developed friendships over thirty years, and I hoped to find a woman who also had best friendships, so we could blend our friends together. Personal growth work had improved the quality of my life noticeably and it's a path I feel I'll always be on; I felt that meeting a woman who had done similar work would enable us to resolve the relationship issues that would invariably arise. That was my list, and it worked, since I did actually meet a woman who enjoyed the same interests. Of course there's also physical chemistry, which can't be determined until meeting in person, but fortunately that turned out to be the icing on the cake.

When someone insists they don't need a list because they'll just know the right person when they meet them, I feel obligated to inform them that the odds against that are overwhelmingly long. Not having a list suggests that you can't articulate who you are, in terms of your own qualities and desires, and therefore can't articulate what you're looking for in a partner. Absent a list as a minimum starting point, you'll waste a lot of time and energy and diminish your chances for success.

Bigger Isn't Always Better

Okay, you made a list, you went online, and you found that the number of potential date candidates that fit your tightly defined parameters has narrowed the field significantly. That was the point, so it's okay if only a handful met your specific needs. It's to be expected, since you're unique, and you want to meet someone whose uniqueness matches yours. Since you only needed to find a few appropriate people to date anyway, and the small number of profiles that popped up met your parameters, the odds are reasonably good that you will find at least a few intriguing dates. After a few emails and a phone call or two, you and your potential date interest have decided to meet for coffee, which is a smart first date choice, since it allows you the freedom to enjoy the date and look forward to another. Alternatively, you'll be glad you didn't waste a lot of time if your date isn't a good match after all, and you had the freedom to say thanks, but no thanks, and leave.

Date Fatigue

Your fantasies are going to have to wait until you actually meet, court, and fall in love with someone. That's the hardest part, since everyone who has ever dated for an extended period of time, reports becoming afflicted with the three F's, Frustration, Fatigue, and Failure. Surely there must be some ways to obviate at least some amount of the affect of the three "F's." There is, and it's imperative boomers know their way around a first date, if they hope to avoid at least some of the potential landmines. If you've gone out with someone four or five times, and you still can't decide if there's relationship potential with that person, you're not dating consciously or intelligently. It's not that complicated. You're going to have to get past your first date jitters, and pay close attention, if you want to avoid dating an inappropriate person several times, and suffer additional three F's, i.e., self-inflicted wounds.

You're sitting in a café drinking coffee, waiting for your date to arrive. His or her online photo was small, since that's all most dating websites can accommodate, although most have a feature that magnifies photos now. You only have a hazy sense of your date's physical appearance. Boomer guys dream about meeting a fantasy version of Diane Keaton, a perky, pretty, smart, in-shape woman. Boomer women want to meet their fantasy version of George Clooney, a handsome, well-spoken, in-shape guy with a terrific sense of humor.

We all know that life rarely works exactly like we'd hoped, but if we're fortunate, and keep our wits about us, we can find someone that may actually, closely resemble our fantasy. We may get stuck on the physical plane sometimes, because that's our first take when meeting someone new. Even if we try not to have first date fantasies, we still likely look at the man or woman sitting across from us in the café, and think about what it might be like to wake up next to that person. Maybe that's a guy thing, but I don't think women are immune from these sorts of thoughts either.

Let me state what I believe is an ideal location for a good first date, no matter how excited and enthusiastic you're feeling about meeting someone. A coffee date is preferable to lunch, dinner, a long walk, a hike, a day at the beach, a picnic, a movie, or any activity that exceeds thirty to sixty minutes. Why? Fair question.

An Interview

A first date is intended as a brief interview, and its main purpose is to determine whether or not a second date is warranted. Some boomers think that categorizing a date, as an interview isn't romantic. Perhaps not, but if it isn't an interview, then what is it? No one should ever consider the notion of falling in love on a first date as smart dating, especially boomers, who should know better. Unless you want to waste your time dating the wrong person for weeks or months, consider a coffee date an interview. That's it, and any expectations beyond that are going to disappoint, because a first-time meeting feels too pressured to be anything more.

Since the majority of first dates don't lead to second dates, let alone relationships, and typically range from "very interesting" to "get me out of here," getting corralled for longer than it takes to decide if you like this person sufficient to see them again, is a mistake. The best possible outcome at the end of a first date is that you'll feel sad it's over, and you'll look eagerly forward to a second date. The worst outcome is that you'll be grateful you didn't waste hours with someone who didn't have real potential. Be cool, calm, and collected, and you'll spare yourself a lot of wasted energy and disappointment.

Think of meeting someone for the first time in terms of feeling enthusiastic to know more about that person, as opposed to driving home in love. Don't project any fantasies onto your date. Keep your wits about you and you'll be able to see the actual person, instead of creating a fantasy. Dating fatigue can make a good date appear larger in your rear view mirror, which means you may be feeling open to anyone that seems even remotely appropriate. Don't become a victim of your fantasies and fatigue.

I typically arrived for a coffee date a few minutes early, so I could watch my date walk into the café. The first thing I noticed was her physical charm, which had little to do with beauty. It was more about whether or not her online photo realistically portrayed how she actually looked. Second, was whether or not she smiled when we made eye contact and we waved to each other. A woman who smiled was always pretty in my eyes, because her smile suggested openness, and a positive attitude about meeting me. I watched her as she walked towards me, and noticed whether she appeared overly nervous. Sure, we're all somewhat nervous on a first date, but I'm an outgoing, Type A guy, and I was looking for an outgoing, Type A woman. I could usually notice that Type A quality in a woman by how she carried herself. If a woman didn't smile when our eyes met, I hoped she'd smile when I got up to greet her.

A date that didn't smile at all was almost always a pass. If someone who has an interest in me, and didn't smile during our date, I doubted she was going to smile much later either. Since I'm a positive, glass half full kind of guy, I wanted to meet a woman with the same qualities. Smiling is natural to most, but not all people, even when meeting for the first time. Remember that a first date is an interview, and just as in any type of interview, smiling is essential. A beaming face is an openhearted gesture, and unless the person's photo totally misrepresented how they look in real life, you want to smile back to show you're pleased to meet them too. No games.

Date Smart: Use a Coffee Date Wisely

I strongly urge boomers to make a first date a coffee date, during the day, and at a busy public café, for several reasons. First, a crowded café buzzing with conversation, actually provides some amount of anonymity and privacy, because the ambient noise masks your conversation, but more important is the safety factor.

Remember, a coffee date is only intended to be a brief introduction so feeling sorry because it felt like it ended too quickly is the best possible outcome. Think in terms of anticipation for the second date, because if you allow that anticipation to build, you'll be chomping at the bit to see that person again. Alternatively, if the date isn't going well you can politely offer that you don't feel there's relationship potential, say thank you, and leave.

Besides your list of qualities, which you used as a guide to choose your online date, there are also the six questions a boomer man or woman should pose on their first date that will help determine if they have the ingredients for a second one. Remember, this is a six for six situation, not the best three or five out of six. I realize that between making your list and asking these questions that it might feel like a prohibitive amount of vetting, but considering that you're interviewing for a life partner, who you'll wake up to every morning, it's a more than worthwhile effort. Remember, you deserve nothing less than someone who can respond with 100% appropriate answers to the six questions. Your strength of character and self-esteem should make this a straightforward decision, because this isn't the part of getting to know someone that involves cutting him or her some slack. You'll thank yourself for your diligence when you meet the man or woman you feel confident about, because you didn't waste time with anyone who wasn't up to your standard.

Remember When Your Teacher Said, "Pay Attention"

If you're paying close attention to the person sitting across from you in the café, you shouldn't find it difficult to decide if a second date is warranted. There are many reasons why making the right decision remains challenging, not the least of which, is the overarching desire many single boomers have to be in a relationship. But we're boomers, and we don't have the six months to a year to waste in a bad relationship, before it becomes so painful that ending it feels like a relief. Repeating the same mistakes when choosing partners indicates desperation, an inability to consciously choose appropriately, having rescue fantasies, or stubbornly insisting on remaining clueless.

Never act out of desperation. If you're feeling desperate, then for heaven's sake don't date for as long as it takes to discover the reasons why. Talk with your closest, most trusted friends who have a personal stake in your happiness and wellbeing. Ask what they did when they were dating and felt hopeless. Take a timeout until you've worked through your feelings of neediness. Remember that the goal is to find a partner who is your equal in every way.

If you follow the suggestions in this chapter, you'll make better choices. And please don't worry that your date will be annoyed by your asking questions. A man or woman who can answer your questions satisfactorily won't be offended, and in fact, they'll appreciate that you're concerned about choosing appropriately.

Chapter Nine:
The Second Date

A Mostly Ignored Topic

I've already shared how to decide who gets a first date, and what that first date might look like, in terms of making it a defining moment. While there is a quite a bit of information about first dates, some useful, some ridiculous, there isn't much written about second dates. I feel second dates are where the boomer dating rubber meets the road. For most boomers, making the decision about who gets a second shot usually turns into a guessing game. This chapter will take most of the guesswork out of an important decision. Ask any boomer who's dating, what's in short supply, and time is most often their answer. We're boomers, and we don't have any to waste so dating smart is key.

Beat and Upbeat

Maybe you're feeling your date passed your first date test with flying colors. It was probably over coffee and, if it was typical it lasted an hour or less, which felt like the perfect amount of time. You enjoyed each other's company, and you're both hoping that your dating lives may have taken a turn for the better. You're smiling at the end of the date because you're feeling relieved that it went so well, and since it's over, you may need some time to figure out what just happened. The pressure you felt, that was connected with your hopes and dreams about meeting someone special, has diminished, and so has a fair amount of your energy. Feeling tired at the end of a first date is normal. You used up lots of adrenalin, and, in the words of Jackson Browne's 1977 hit, you're "Running on Empty".

Narrow the Field

My second date track record was less than stellar in terms of numbers, but as I consistently state, dating isn't a numbers game. Out of nearly fifty women I met for coffee dates over a two-year period I had just six, second dates. Was I being picky? Of course I was. I wasn't looking for dates. I wanted to meet my life-partner, and when I considered the viability of a second date on that basis, it was easy to decide. There's no compromising involved when choosing a life partner. That's worth repeating. Think in terms of sitting across the breakfast table with the same man or woman every morning for the rest of your life without regretting your choice. You deserve the perfect partner.

There was nothing wrong with most of the women I didn't second dates. Many had much of what I was looking for, and I felt chemistry with a few. But I wanted the whole package, and I knew from the many years I'd dated, that I wasn't going to be satisfied in a relationship with a woman who didn't light me up in every possible way. This is the magic I've mentioned before. It's real; please don't think it's not, or that you'll never experience it. Everyone can and should. Remember, it's not only a fantasy found exclusively in romance novels and movies.

Your Rain Gauge

Hopefully you already asked all or most of the six first date questions I suggested in the First Date chapter, and you're using the answers to help you determine who gets a second date. I can't emphasize too strongly how important it is to ask these questions, and any others you know in your heart are deal killers, if they aren't answered satisfactorily. There's no rain gauge for dating, no measuring device to help you decide, so beyond asking critical questions, there's no useful tool for second date appropriateness, except the one that connects your head with your heart. A man or woman who answered your questions to your satisfaction has earned second date consideration. They've shown some mettle, and demonstrated that they haven't been mentally or emotionally unconscious for the past few decades. Is it rare to find this person? While they're not ubiquitous, contrary to popular boomer wisdom, I don't believe good candidates are rare. But it's impossible to know with any certainty unless you ask the right questions, which will give you at least some basis in reality for making a second date decision.

You may need to give some boomer dates the benefit of the doubt, in terms of whether or not they were completely relaxed with you, which doesn't mean they get a pass, in terms of how they answered your questions. After spending decades in a relationship, with a partner who unfortunately, didn't turn out to be your date's Mr. or Mrs. Right, it may feel awkward for them to relate to you on a romantic level right away. Sure, it would be terrific if every boomer man or woman you meet swept you off your feet, but if you decide someone has solid relationship potential, you may have to wait a bit before you feel swept. Besides, the notion of being swept off your feet is flawed anyway. The word swept suggests not having sufficient time to feel what's really happening. A better term for love at first sight is lust at first sight. We're boomers and we should know the difference.

Is a second date a good idea after hearing the right answers to your questions, and feeling some amount of chemistry? Sure, and the sooner the better. There's no reason to play any games at this stage of life. Rules that younger daters follow, like how many days to wait before calling after a first date, and a host of other nonsensical tricks and gimmicks, don't work for boomers. In truth, they don't work for anyone else either.

A Pregnant Pause

When the first date was over, and it was time to leave the café, you may have looked at each other with uncertainty about what to do next. Should you say something about another date or just let it go for the time being? Being cool isn't really what you should be thinking about, and saying or not saying anything is usually more about not knowing what to say in that moment than anything else.

Boomers who haven't dated in a while may find this sudden moment of silence perplexing, bordering on the uncomfortable. Either someone says something about another date or both people will just get up and leave. While this isn't dating when you were younger, there aren't any rules regarding who suggests the second date. There were times when I was unsure, and I felt greatly relieved when a date asked if I'd like to see her again. That kind of honest directness always appealed to me. The truth is that feeling pursued feels good when there's a spark between a man and a woman. Who should do the pursuing isn't necessarily gender specific.

Contrary to what many boomer women may think, most men appreciate a woman who is somewhat bold and up front about saying what she wants. Strength of character is a very attractive quality, and it has nothing to do with traditional gender roles. When I was interested in a woman and she asked me out for a second date, she immediately went to the top of my list. Boomer women might consider that even the right man may be feeling shy or reluctant to take a chance and ask a woman for a second date. He's got all the qualities a woman was hoping to find, but he's a little slow off the mark. His speed doesn't point to his level of masculinity, and it's more likely related to his fear that you'll say no. Rejection isn't something many of us handle well in any social situation, and dating is no exception.

There's another issue at the end of a first date that frequently ends up causing women to feel they've been treated unfairly. The most commonly repeated three words that men utter at the end of a first date, whether they mean them or not, are "I'll call you." I struggled not to say this when I didn't mean it, and from numerous comments I've received over the years, it appears that lots of other men struggle with how to best end a first date, when a second isn't what they want.

Men Mostly Mean Well

While it may not always be apparent or believable, men honestly don't like to disappoint. Pleasing is in our male DNA. Telling a woman he'll call her doesn't necessarily mean that man will. It's a painless exit from a date, and one that avoids looking a woman in the eye and telling her the truth, which might be, thanks but no thanks. I always convinced myself I was sparing a woman's feelings by telling her I'd call when I didn't mean it, but the truth was I was only sparing my own feelings. I avoided feeling uncomfortable by being less than honest. Okay this isn't a horrible lie, but it also isn't appropriate. This is a defining, manning up moment, and guys might consider the importance of rising to the occasion and being forthright.

I'm not suggesting women should assume the role of asking men for a second date, but rather that when a woman asks a man for a second date, it may elicit a more authentic response. It takes all the pressure off a guy when his date takes the risk and asks him out. I know, that's not how women generally like to be romanced, but we're seasoned, and we accept that we aren't always suave and sophisticated. If a woman likes a guy and wants to see him again after the date is over, it's okay if she asks him first. It may be that he simply isn't feeling a sufficiently strong footing yet.

What's Pacing?

Assuming both people feel a second date is mutually desired, what's that date supposed to look like? This section is about pacing. Pacing comes into play as a relationship issue right from the beginning. It's rare when both people feel the exact same pacing. Pacing is the speed at which people feel comfortable getting to know the other person, and moving the relationship to the next level. It's not gender-driven by any means. Men and women struggle equally with pacing, and need to know how to talk about it in order to make their differences in speed work. Too many budding relationships die on the vine unnecessarily because pacing was different, and neither person recognized it was an issue that could be worked through with patience and understanding.

Our culture is locked on a permanent high speed setting for everything. Instant oatmeal, two-minute car washes, microwave dinners, ten-minute oil changes, fast food restaurants, and instant online purchasing, are all speed-related activities. So naturally that need for speed must translate into relationships, right? And a second date always signifies the beginning of a relationship, right? Wrong on both counts. Nearly every boomer has figured out that nothing worthwhile in life ever comes easily or quickly, and that pertains especially to relationships.

Some boomers are obsessed with closing the relationship deal quickly, which means elevating their new love interest to the lofty position of permanent partner, immediately. What's clear about their rushed attitude is that they prefer to skip the getting to know you process completely. They're demonstrating an unrealistic, premature desire to move the relationship up to the next level. This is nearly always a mistake. Speeding up the pace typically leads to couples becoming sexual too soon, which becomes an ill-fated, self-fulfilling prophecy for failure in nearly every brand new relationship. When couples can't find firm ground ,and believe that sex will steady their relationship and bring them closer, quicker, their relationship runs off the rails and everyone gets hurt.

Life as Lego

Becoming sexual too early in a relationship circumvents the getting to know you process, only to discover a few months later that the relationship never had any basis in reality. There are many reasons why men and women may be so unrealistically quick off the mark. When two people have diametrically opposing senses of pacing, trouble nearly always follows. Some men and women are addicted to love at first sight, which inevitably morphs into a rocket ride. They seem unwilling to remember that those rockets always crash and burn, and that the pain that follows lingers for a long time. Think of a second date in terms of a starting gate for building a lasting relationship. You can't cobble a relationship together hastily and hope it will last. It won't.

There's no dragging someone kicking and screaming into deepening a relationship, just because you feel it's inevitable and there's no sense wasting time. The time spent getting to know someone is never wasted. It's a precious time of discovery that can't be rushed or skipped. It's typically the more experienced boomer daters who are aware that the differences in pacing between two people can be problematic. After a failed relationship, many boomers feel a palpable hunger to be paired again, and the more time that has elapsed since that relationship ended, the more that feeling of anxiety can lead to unrealistic expectations. Resist the temptation to fall in love before spending ample time getting to know the other person. Rushing into love means projecting who you want the other person to be, rather than seeing that person for whom they really are. Keep in mind that projections are nearly always wrong.

So a perfect second date means dinner at a restaurant or your date's home, right? Not necessarily. That's probably rushing it, considering that dinner is better reserved as the start of a romantic evening with someone for whom you've developed at least minimal feelings. Keeping the pressure off is the best way to get to know someone, and what form a second date takes has a lot to do with how that's accomplished. Go slow. Dinner with your new love interest feels best when it's a celebration acknowledging the beginning of what you both feel might be the end of your dating careers.

Dinner is looking at your date with a sense of hope born from knowing that person more than casually, because you took time to get acquainted. Dinner is feeling confident there's a strong possibility you have a future together. While dinner has become a common second date, and boomer men seemingly can't wait to take women out to dinner, it's not necessarily the smartest second date choice. Maybe it's because men have traditionally been deal-closers, and it's our nature to want to wine and dine women and have them fall in love with us. I remember dating a woman who told me to slow down because she wasn't a business deal to close. She was right.

Venue Choices

A long walk is a perfect second date because it affords plenty of time to talk, and the opportunity to get to know each other better in an unpressured atmosphere. Resist the temptation to project the finish of the race while you're still at the starting gate. Just relax, and see if you can ascertain if relationship potential is real or imagined. Taking a walk isn't pressured, no one has to dress up, and it can be a delightful, relaxed time together. It's sweet when both people feel like holding hands. I remember a second date walk when I reached for my date's hand. She yanked it away hard, and said bluntly that she thought holding hands was for teenagers. I was shocked by her lack of warmth, and grateful our date ended after a short walk instead of a long dinner.

Assuming that both people are feeling closer and equally interested in each other after a walk, sharing a spontaneous lunch is a perfect end to a second date. The more you slow the getting to know you process down, the better you'll actually get to know each other. I realize this sounds simplistic, but considering how frequently people rush into relationships it seems worth mentioning. Alternatively a bicycle ride, a hike, a rowboat around a lake, or any activity that's done in pleasant surroundings, allows for conversation, and can work well. Unlike a restaurant, a walk is an opportunity to talk privately, and you won't have to raise your voice to be heard. A picnic afterward can feel as romantic as lunch at a restaurant, and is far more private. A successful second date means reducing the pressure to as close to zero as possible.

Anticipation

Heinz ran a commercial on television years ago showing an upside down ketchup bottle slowly pouring its contents, while playing a song about anticipation in the background. The point of their commercial was that their ketchup was so good that it was worth waiting for. Similarly anticipation in relationships is worth waiting for, and should be enjoyed.

Anticipation has the power to imbue the sweet sense that something wonderful is happening between two people. It's been described as tingling, exciting, promising, and in many other ways. It should be enjoyed for as long as possible because it feels wonderful; enjoy it and don't skip past it prematurely. The slower a couple moves their relationship along the getting to know you path, the more certain both partners will feel about taking it to the next level.

Feeling high after your second time together is special, but don't mistake that special feeling for love. Infatuation usually precedes love, and it's not something you want to skip either, since it's the beginning that each of you will always remember. Rushing through the getting to know you process is wrong, no matter how good you're feeling about the other person. Anticipation means allowing the magic to grow and cast its spell. It's just too grand to rush.

If you feel you've found your life partner on your second date, I suggest you keep that feeling to yourself, because the other person's pacing may be considerably slower than yours. Pacing doesn't have to become a problem, and it won't hurt a fledgling relationship if each person's timing is respected. Just because you're feeling sure your second date with a man or woman is a clincher, doesn't mean the other person necessarily shares your excitement. Anticipation is best enjoyed when it goes hand in hand with patience and respect. There's no reason that the getting to know you process should be viewed as anything but fun. I learned this lesson late in life, but learning it has saved me countless months in the wrong relationships.

Continue to ask questions that you may have forgotten to ask on your first date, and remember that with few exceptions, not much is out of bounds. Particularly ask about your dates' relationship history, not with the purpose of judging them, but rather to discover what they've gleaned about their failed relationships. It takes two people to make or break a relationship, and that means your date should take his or her share of the responsibility for their failed relationship's demise. There are terrific lessons to be gleaned from failure, but they're lost unless they're owned.

Sometimes a second date is disappointing, and that's usually because one or both people listened to the answers to their questions, but perhaps didn't hear them on a cognitive level. Worse, they most likely made the fatal mistake of projecting, which leads to unrealistic expectations. Okay, dust yourself off, forgive yourself, and remember not to caught-up in projecting next time, but to listening with rapt attention instead.

A Gateway

A second date can be the gateway to a relationship if it's handled well. The purpose of a second date is to continue getting to know the other person, not to begin making a wedding invitation list. A third date and beyond will depend entirely on the success of the second. Knowing when to get into, or walk away from a relationship can be challenging, and no one wants to miss a potentially wonderful life partner.

Continuing a relationship isn't solely a heart decision. There needs to be some rational thought given to the other person's suitability as a partner. Is this man or woman someone you feel you might be able to create a life with? It shouldn't take months to determine this if you're paying attention rather than projecting.

The most important second date rule is the same as the first date rule. GO SLOW because you'll only be able to determine the other person's viability as a partner if you take your time. Resist the temptation to strap on a rocket and blast off with someone you don't really know yet. The crash and burn phase of that ride makes it a penalty you definitely want to avoid. How many rocket rides do you honestly feel you have left in your psyche, before you give up searching for a life partner and walk away from dating, frustrated and hopeless? It was the crashed and burned rockets that hurt every time I became embroiled in a bad relationship that finally opened my eyes to the truth. I was always in a hurry to fall in love and settle into a relationship with a woman, and my anxiety was connected with boyhood abandonment issues I hadn't faced yet. Smart dating doesn't eliminate every problem, but it's important to remember that hurrying into the wrong relationship can be avoided just by slowing down.

If you consider a second date as a pleasant time to share with someone you're interested in getting to know better, instead of trying to predict the future with that person, you'll be more likely to glean what you need to know from it. You don't want to waste months in a relationship that you know in your heart will never work. You can easily avoid making this mistake by taking all the time you need to discover the authentic person you're dating. Falling in love comes after you've been completely honest with yourself about what you're getting into, and in particular with whom you're getting into it. While it may seem difficult in the moment, try to enjoy your second date. It's one you and your partner will hopefully recollect for years with a sense of joy.

Chapter Ten:
Sexual Intimacy

Beginning to be sexual again, after a long-term relationship, is a double-edged sword. Sure, there's a lot of pent-up sexual desire and you want to act on that, but there's some fear associated with it too. Months, years, or longer without great sex or no sex at all, may leave a boomer feeling needy but nervous about their sexuality. The good news is muscle memory: sex is like riding a bicycle. The bad news is that great sex doesn't necessarily just happen because ours was the free love generation. That's no longer a viable sexual path for boomers.

Before becoming sexual again, it's smart to examine your sexual history, in terms of whether or not you enjoyed sex, and the reasons why you did or didn't. It's not uncommon for a boomer not to have enjoyed sex, and this becomes obvious when talking with boomers about their sexuality. "I can live without it," suggests sex was never great, because if it was there wouldn't be any willingness to give it up. It also suggests that sex and a strong emotional attachment, may have never been in the same room at the same time.

Not a Happy Ending

I had a sexual epiphany at the end of my first, post-divorce date, with a woman I'd met online. We were standing at her front door having an awkward moment, with neither of us knowing what to do next. She broke the clumsy silence by inviting me in for a drink. I didn't know what to expect, but she'd flirted with me during the evening in ways a man never fails to recognize. During dinner, she'd lightly stroked my arm and left her hand on top of mine, and after dinner when I helped her on with her coat, she brushed her cheek against my hand and held it there long enough to send me an unmistakable message. In addition to her physical touch, the scent of her perfume was intoxicating. It felt so sweet to be with a woman again. While her acts of affection were reassuring, I didn't consider sex on our first date likely. Still, I felt sexually alive in a manner I hadn't in a long while.

We began kissing passionately and deeply the moment the door shut behind us. My heart was pounding so rapidly I thought it would burst through my chest. All I could think about was how desperately I wanted and needed to feel like a man again. I'd never been celibate prior my failed marriage, and the lack of sex had played a major role in its demise. When my date ran her lips over my neck, her hot breath made me lose all sense of self-control, and when she began rubbing her body against mine I became so aroused I honestly couldn't think straight. After a few moments, she took me by the hand like a lost little boy and led me to her bedroom. The roar from my wildly beating heart thundered in my ears deafening me, and my mouth became so dry I could barely swallow. We hadn't spoken a single word since we began kissing, but the sexual energy between us was palpable, unmistakable, and unrelenting. We were definitely going to have sex.

She yanked her sweater over her head and tore her jeans off so quickly they were both inside out when she threw them on the bedroom floor. She stood in front of me in white lace bra and panties, her face glowing with sexual desire beyond hot and inviting. Suddenly, my lustful desire did a shocking 180. Kate was 60, toned, tanned, beautiful, and panting hard; the shift in my mood was related neither to her beauty or her willingness.

A few, mood-killing thoughts had begun racing through my head. I was already worrying I wouldn't be able to perform. Sure, I'd been celibate for a while, but I hadn't engaged in casual sex in a decade, and since I hadn't anticipated first date sex, I hadn't brought condoms. But the truth was that condoms weren't the issue. It just felt wrong-headed to be sexually intimate with a woman I hardly knew, who was eager to have sex with a guy she didn't know either.

This was in total conflict with my sexual history. Instead of jumping at the opportunity to have sex with a beautiful woman, I was stuck worrying about being sexually dysfunctional, something I'd rarely considered before. No longer aroused, I backed away from her, backing toward the bedroom door. I felt caught between shame and confusion. "What's wrong?" she asked, sitting down on her bed, visibly shaken by my sudden retreat. "I'll call you," I trailed behind me as I turned around and nearly ran through the door, but I knew I wouldn't. While she was into casual sex, my involuntary response had pointedly indicated I wasn't.

Something inside me had flipped since I was single and sexual last. I couldn't remember ever turning down a woman's offer of sex. But I knew a stranger couldn't satisfy the hunger I was feeling in my heart. The nature of my sexuality seemed to have changed without my permission or approval. Even in a desperate moment, when I felt incredibly aroused, casual sex suddenly seemed like a Band-Aid. I wanted more than that, much more. I wanted to experience sex and love together. I get that this is fairly basic for lots of boomers, but this was a new feeling for me.

I'd been fantasizing about falling in love since my divorce, and my abrupt retreat from an opportunity for casual sex reinforced that fantasy. I'd spent most of my dating years engaging in sex that was mostly devoid of emotion, and that had left me jaded about sex with a stranger. It dawned on me after my first, post-divorce date, that I wanted a deep heart connection with a woman, but didn't know how to deal with the fear I'd always associated with that. I had long-running trust issues, and my recent sexual misadventure demonstrated that I needed to be in a meaningful relationship, in order to put my trust issues behind me. I wanted to feel love in my heart, not just my head, while making love. I admit that some of my new attitude about casual sex was related to getting older, but I also hoped I might be getting smarter. I put casual sex behind me after this date, and I never looked back.

It Wasn't My Thing. It Was a Guy Thing

After talking with other recently divorced boomer men, I discovered that my lack of enthusiasm for casual sex wasn't as rare as I'd first thought. Sure, I'd read more than a thousand comments from women about my first date sex articles in *The Huffington Post,* and most said they were weary and wary of boomer guys expecting first date sex. It was clear that some boomer guys were still fans of casual sex, but none of the men I knew were. I was still struggling with a painful sense of loss, and deep-seated feelings of failure from my divorce. I knew if I ignored this new feeling about being in love, before making love, I'd regret it.

A conflict had developed in my male psyche related to casual sex, which I'd glibly accepted as part of my manhood and my reality. But casual sex had never resulted in a long-term relationship for me. No matter how hard I tried, I couldn't conjure up any reasons why the results would be different now. But there was another issue I was also struggling with. I was afraid I'd be dating indefinitely, which was a powerful fear to face in my sixties. I didn't know any sixty-something guys who still loved dating, including me. I wanted my next relationship to be my last. To make this possible I needed to learn how to connect my heart with my head. While that may seem simple, and maybe even juvenile to most boomers, it meant defeating my trust demons, which had held my heart in a vice-like grip since boyhood.

Casual sex had only partially filled the emptiness and feelings of loneliness, that had burdened me since I was a boy, but now I felt casual sex was more masturbation than actual sex. I had painted over my loneliness with momentary sexual pleasure, which had never assuaged my sadness. Like most newly single guys, I was eager to date and become sexual again. When my body needed sex, my head had always been amenable. But I knew with certainty that I'd feel worse if I reverted to casual sex.

My changing sexuality seemed new and difficult to implement, but I couldn't ignore the paradigm shift just because it was going to be challenging. Giving in to my sexual urges by engaging in casual sex again would be self-sabotaging. Still, those urges had always pushed me toward having sex with any willing woman. My strong sense that I'd be hurting myself if I acquiesced was enough to counter my libido, and in the end my sensibility prevailed. I admit I was surprised the extent to which my libido still had a powerful influence in my sixties. It seemed like a primitive instinct I'd always be struggling with. Thankfully it turned out not to be.

Whether you're a man or a woman, you and your ex likely stopped being sexual long before you decided to divorce. Nothing kills a sexual moment like a knockdown argument, and in most failed marriages the fighting never seems to end. Even though making love is muscle memory, we all feel somewhat rusty about sex after a long dry spell. The one thing every recently divorced boomer man and woman can agree on is that none wants to suffer through the painful breakup process again. While I can't guarantee you won't, I promise that the likelihood you'll experience that pain again will be decreased substantially, if you follow your heart and not just your head.

Think Outside the Box

Decades of working with men in small groups, in addition to dating boomer women, showed me that while many boomers aren't particularly skilled at connecting with each other on a heart level, it's primarily men who find that connection the most difficult to make. What I know with absolute certainty, is that if you're a boomer man or woman who hopes to be in a relationship that includes The Best Sex Imaginable, TBSI, you're going to have to fully invest your heart in your partner first. The difference between casual sex, which is good at best, and TBSI, which is incredible, is the power of the sexual energy inherent in a loving relationship that embodies absolute trust.

The reason that trust is so critical for TBSI is that it's only after two people trust each partner unconditionally that each can feel safe enough to be completely sexually vulnerable. What does sexual vulnerability mean? Absent unconditional trust, one or both partners will hold back, probably not enough to preclude sex, but enough to make off the charts, vulnerable sex impossible. Boomers who prefer to be sexual without that level of trust can act on their sexual urges, but they won't reach the level of TBSI. Even if this seems like a new concept, it's likely you've felt something was missing in the sexual aspect of past relationships; what may have been missing was unconditional trust. I hope to assure every man and woman starting a new relationship, that by fully investing your hearts, making love can reach the pinnacle, TBSI.

Engage My Heart? Ouch!

Boomers can have sex like they did decades ago, but not by relying entirely on their bodies any longer. If they hope to have TBSI they're going to have to engage their hearts. Hold on. Don't leave yet, guys, it's not what you think. Before I was 50, women hadn't expected much in the way of emotional dialogue or connection, before sex or after, which was good since I didn't have much to offer. After 50, I noticed the relationship paradigm beginning to shift. Women wanted me to talk about my feelings in the context of a relationship before sex.

When I hit 55, suddenly and without warning I found myself struggling to maintain an erection during sex. I panicked. Casual sex, which was eminently doable the day before, wasn't possible today. I thought my libido might be in decline and that my sex life might actually have an expiration date. I had my testosterone level checked. Normal. Okay now what?

I considered giving up in shame and defeat. The notion of sex with an emotional component was brand new and daunting. I'd always assumed my sexual virility would last for as long as I did. I mustered the courage to talk about my problem with a few close men friends, who suggested that the heart/peter connection was critical to their sexual performance and enjoyment. I didn't argue since they were all in long-term sexually hot relationships.

Since I was terrified to attempt this emotional high-wire dialogue with a woman right away, I practiced talking about my feelings with the same guys who were in great sexual relationships. When they asked me question relating to how I felt, and I answered with what I thought instead, they reminded me that they didn't care what I thought, but rather what I was feeling in that moment.

This was frustrating and humbling, especially since I'd gotten away with never talking about my feelings with women, or with men either for that matter. Sometimes I'd leave my friends feeling discouraged, and I'd think, "Ahh, screw it. I don't need this shit." But then I remembered that I wasn't ready to give sex up yet, and I'd sit alone at home and practice noticing the difference between how I felt, and what I thought. In a month or so, I became marginally proficient. In a few months, I felt ready to share my feelings with a woman.

The moment of truth came shortly after meeting a woman I liked, and with whom I had strong sexual feelings. She was adamant on our first date that sex was off limits, unless or until we had an emotional connection. Fortunately she was as patient with me as my men friends had been, and as I fell in love with her I discovered I could tell her so and mean it. I trusted her with my heart, which took all the courage I could muster. When we finally fell into bed my sexual problem was magically resolved. I was cured, amazed, grateful, and anxious to get the word out to other boomer men. Our relationship lasted until she moved out of the country. Lesson learned.

Advanced BSI

I had achieved my goal, which was to be able to maintain an erection and enjoy a higher quality sex, but I began to feel that this shouldn't be my ultimate goal. I listened to men who were still having TBSI with their partners after decades. I knew there was a higher sexual plateau than the one I had recently reached, and I wanted to get there. I wanted to perform like a young lion again. Yeah, I was taking Cialis occasionally in my late 60's, but I knew that was only a partial solution. ED pills keep it up, but they don't get it up. Only a deeper heart connection was going to make me a lion again.

I realized that the complete experience required finding a woman with whom I resonated, like two tuning forks, humming in perfect pitch with each other. This search proved far more elusive than getting in touch with my feelings. This appeared to be the proverbial needle in the haystack. Never believe anyone who tells you that finding your ultimate life and sex partner is easy. This goes well beyond compatibility, which is a word that conjures up my relationship with my golden retriever. Compatibility isn't nearly enough, in terms of having TBSI. Compatibility is the low hanging fruit that isn't the sweetest just because it's the easiest to pick.

What's a TBSI Partner Look Like?

How would I know this perfect woman if I were lucky enough to meet her? What would she look like? Would she resemble my traditional type? It took four-dozen coffee dates, and a few discombobulating, false starts before I met the woman with whom I was able to perform like a young lion again. The big surprise was that she was nothing at all like any of the women I'd known previously.

She was tall, which wasn't my customary type, and she was beautiful in an ethnic, natural way, that had nothing to do with a perfect ski jump nose, glitzy makeup, or a designer wardrobe. She had a thin, angular face, and a very prominent nose, which oddly made me feel crazy with desire. Her slender body, narrow hips, and small derriere, excited me every time she walked by. In addition, and most importantly, her temperament, personality, and sexuality, were soft, sweet, and hot, in that order. Making love with her became the lightening bolt of film and romance novel renown. This was what I always thought of as magic, in terms of meeting the "one." The bromide, you can't teach old dogs new tricks, isn't true. We simply need to look beyond our customary types. What does that mean? Look at the next man or woman you meet as if he or she is the first man or woman you've ever seen, and you'll notice things that you've been missing in men and women for as long as you've dated.

My New Best Friend

From our second date, which was dinner at a Vietnamese restaurant, we laughed and played together effortlessly, as if we'd been friends for years. Our emotional connection grew like a weed, and we talked about it frequently. I felt safe with her, and knew I could share how I felt about her, and our relationship without fear. Our time together became magical; if you haven't experienced magic don't discount it. But you won't find magic if you're in a relationship that doesn't include it. You'll know when you've found it, because you'll feel lightheaded, sexually charged to the nth degree, and you'll be smiling all day for no apparent reason.

Is sex an important part of boomer relationships? It's nothing less than a critical component. Feeling regret is a waste of time, particularly since being involved in a less than stellar sexual relationship is avoidable. No matter how old you are, don't ever think you're over the hill sexually, or that it's ever too late to enjoy TBSI. It happened for my partner and me in our sixties, and we're not an anomaly. It's your right, so don't cheat yourself out of the decades you have left to enjoy such great sex that you won't want it to end. And this is important, don't beat yourself up for missing out on BSI for so long. Just appreciate that you've discovered it in time to enjoy it. Fall in love, and then fall into bed, with the man or woman of your dreams.

Casual Sex = Masturbation

Let me talk with boomer men for a moment. Like it or not the quality of sex after fifty is inexorably linked to the level of emotional connection in our relationships. Nearly every boomer guy could get laid in the 60's and 70's, because women were as willing to engage in casual sex as we were. Remember sex, drugs, and rock and roll? While everyone didn't necessarily do drugs, very few didn't like sex, and finding a willing partner didn't take much finesse.

Boomer women's attitudes about casual sex have changed considerably since then. Boomer men can either accept that change or be rejected, because most women are willing to wait patiently to be in a relationship built on an emotionally driven foundation. But hold on, this isn't the bad news, guys. I'll explain why it isn't.

What I'm suggesting is a far more intensely pleasurable sexual experience than casual sex ever offered. I know that this may sound like a pie in the sky buildup, but indulge me, because I've shared most of the sexual issues men struggle with. In truth, I discovered that having TBSI was linked to a strong emotional connection by accident. When I fell in love with my partner on a heart-connected level, the difference between the quality of casual sex and loving sex astounded me. I'd inadvertently stepped up my sexual game, which was enhanced exponentially. After reading more about TBSI, I hope that all of the men for whom this is new, will consider the value of creating a trusting emotional connection with a woman before becoming sexual. Having the best sex of your life might be worth serious consideration.

In my forties, and into my fifties, I realized I actually felt less satisfied after casual sex than before it, and that this phenomenon had nothing to do with how beautiful or willing my partner was. I frequently satisfied myself when I went home afterward, because casual sex had become unsatisfying. Since sex with my partner is an expression of my love for her, I feel fully satisfied on a physical level after we make love. And since I feel loved, I also feel satisfied on an emotional level. I can actually sense the love in my body, and even though I'm in my late sixties, my sexual performance has improved noticeably.

Boomer guys in particular, need to stop kidding themselves about wanting to get their sexual fantasies fulfilled, particularly fantasies connected with porn, which is a bad road leading nowhere. Porn is a monkey wrench that seems to get thrown into too many relationships with the advent of the Internet, and it has filled some men with unrealistic ideas of what sex is supposed to look like.

The most relevant factor is that porn sexual fantasies aren't based in any reality. There's a world of difference between men being sexually dominant, and women porn stars being okay with sexual abuse on camera. Women in porn are paid to let men abuse them. What's sad is that a high percentage of porn actresses were abused as young girls. A boomer guy who expects a boomer woman to act like a porn star, in terms of abusive, casual sex, is barking up the wrong tree. Male sexual dominance is the norm in many relationships, including mine, and as long as it's mutually agreeable it works. Abusive, porn-like sex fits into an entirely different category.

A man hasn't experienced TBSI unless he's felt unconditional trust for a woman, and vice versa. Loving and trusting a sexual partner makes a world of difference, in terms of the satisfying nature of TBSI, and that also extends to how we feel about our partners and ourselves afterward. To look your partner in their eyes after you've both climaxed and are holding each other, and actually see the love, imparts a level of satisfaction, safety, and sense of longevity, that only loving, trusting sex can provide.

In Defense of Women

Frankly it's clear from thousands of boomer women's comments about boomer men who pressure them for first date sex, that some guys are either unwilling or unable to grasp that most boomer women feel it's wildly inappropriate. In the face of so much resistance from so many women, it should be obvious that pressuring women for first date sex isn't going to succeed very often, and considering the lower sexual satisfaction inherent in casual sex, it doesn't seem like a particularly lofty goal anyway. Pursuing a casual sex agenda with boomer women sets up conflict where none is needed, and it also lends an unnecessarily angry tone to boomer dating. Years ago when I began writing about boomer sex, dating, and relationships I was surprised by the level of anger from women related to the issue of first date sex.

I would suggest boomer men, who insist boomer women are too angry and bitter to date, take a step back and consider how their myopic sexual agendas may contribute to that anger and bitterness. Since this conflict about casual sex completely ignores the lack of quality of sex, and doesn't speak to most women's needs, it seems pointless to pressure women for something that isn't all that good in the first place.

Guys, please consider that the motives of a boomer woman who's amenable to first date sex should actually concern you, not fill you with joy, because she'd be in such a small minority of women, that a man would have to be foolish to think he got lucky. More than likely he's making a huge mistake. What a man should ask himself is why doesn't that woman place any value on the heart/sex connection? Worse, is her willingness to have casual sex just a hook to reel in another unconscious guy? This is a perfect example of being careful what you wish for. Is a boomer woman right to want to be in a relationship and know a man on an emotionally intimate basis before sharing her body with him? Sure she is, and especially if she wants to enjoy TBSI, which she is likely aware is linked to a loving, trusting emotional connection.

Being emotionally vulnerable isn't related only to sexual benefits. It's about becoming half of an authentic, caring, nurturing, committed relationship, and the comfort derived from having a partner whose support is unconditional. No fear, remember? I respect the reasons why most boomer women reject casual sex, because they're aware that men who engage in it are doing so simply to satisfy their immediate needs. That's insulting to a boomer woman, because the inherent message is that it's okay to use her to relieve his sexual tension. To ask a woman in her 50's or 60's to sexually satisfy a stranger is demeaning and insulting, and boomer men might consider that they're damaging their own self-esteem by treating women in this manner. That's not a particularly manly position. Savvy, emotionally conscious boomer guys, don't make specious arguments in favor of first date sex, because trying to talk a boomer woman, or any woman for that matter, into having sex, is juvenile and lame.

Conscious men don't use women for sex; they make love to them. Having said this, I regret it took me so long to figure this out. My sexual behavior with women was mechanical and unfeeling for too long, and while some of the women were okay with that, some were not. I urge my fellow boomer guys to reconsider their sexual parameters, particularly those around first date sex.

One man's comment after an article I wrote about the virtues of boomer women in *The Huffington Post* suggested that boomer women must have castrated me because I hold them in such high regard. I responded that I finally grew a pair, which allowed me to appreciate them for their wonderful qualities. Disparaging or abusing women for sexual pleasure is misogyny, which isn't something that should make any man feel proud. It's a destructive sexual philosophy, because that level of domination inflicts emotional and physical damage on women, and men who subscribe to misogyny also damage themselves, and limit their chances of ever enjoying the warmth that is sex with emotional intimacy.

Boomer men, who think that TBSI is entirely related to a woman's beauty, sexual availability, or willingness, probably won't ever get to enjoy it. To enjoy sex at TBSI level, men have to open their hearts. Absent that, men might consider that continuing to ask boomer women who are strangers to satisfy their sexual needs, is really about fear of intimacy. In terms of pleasure it's just a step above masturbation. Boomer women deserve better, and so do boomer men.

That's it guys. I'm urging you to have the best sex you may have ever had. Casual sex has a chronological shelf life in terms of physical performance ability, while TBSI is sustainable for decades to come, and it's your heart connection with a woman that will determine that. Honest.

No Age Limit

I've dated on and off for many years, and a fair amount of that time was spent in relationships. I've been sexual with a lot of women, which is a reference point, not a boast, since it was primarily casual sex, and not the most satisfying. I've paid close attention to women's sexual needs. I still enjoy sex enormously, and at 69, I'm having the TBSI with my 65 year-old sweetheart, who I love and adore in the context of a committed relationship. Every boomer deserves to enjoy sex at stellar heights. Whether or not you've ever been in an unconditionally loving, trusting relationship and experienced TBSI is unimportant, because if you follow a few simple suggestions, you most surely will.

The Ingredients for The Best Sex Imaginable

There are several ingredients for TBSI, which doesn't have any boundaries, rules, or holding back. Since it's totally trusting, it can be wildly adventurous. It embraces the notion that the greatest sex imaginable is loving, and therefore absolutely uninhibited; age is irrelevant. It lives in your head and your heart, and boomers have a myriad of life experiences, that when added to the mix, help create TBSI.

Desire

The degree to which your sexual experience is stellar, depends heavily on the existence of an emotional connection, but it's also linked to physical desirability. This is obvious, right? Perhaps not, when you consider the large percentage of men and women who end up partnering with someone they aren't TBSI hot for. In candor, I've entered into relationships in which TBSI remained out of reach, and my flawed reasons for doing so haunted me well after the relationships were over.

Money, compatibility, loneliness, companionship, desperation, and a myriad of other reasons and excuses are frequently mentioned. In the end, the nearly universal desire men and women have to be in loving, trusting relationships, that are also hot and sexual bubble up, and that's when poor choices in partners make them feel shortchanged. Of all the reasons mentioned, loneliness affected me the most, until I learned the difference between being alone and feeling lonely. You're starting over and you don't need to repeat past mistakes. Be patient, and for your own sake, don't jump into a relationship with the first willing person. Your self-esteem is at stake.

Choose a partner who makes you ache with sexual desire. Nothing less will take you to the sexual heights of TBSI. While this is personal and different for everyone, whatever it is about a man or woman that makes you sexually wild with desire is cool. Some men like skinny women, while others like lots of meat on the bones. Some women like muscular men, while others like leaner guys. It's all, good. Sure, there's an initial honeymoon period when nearly all men and women feel hot for each other, but if you hope to enjoy TBSI, your partner will have to be able to satisfy your sexual fantasies, no matter his or her other qualities. This may sound prohibitive and limiting, but settling for less will more than likely end in frustration and regret. Most of us have been in sexually unsatisfying relationships, and most of us vowed not to repeat this mistake. Remember your resolve, and how sexually frustrated, and perhaps even angry, you felt by the time that relationship ended. That ought to be remind you to stay on the path.

Sexual Knowledge

You owe it to yourself and your partner, to be fully armed with sexual knowledge about your bodies, needs, and the mechanics that make TBSI possible. What drives men and women over the sexual bliss cliff? I'll explain in a bit.

Emotional Connection

If you're a boomer guy, and you still think you have lots of casual sex years ahead of you, think again. You don't. Whether you're a man or woman, your body simply isn't going to support casual sex as you age, and there's nothing sadder than an older man or woman chasing young bodies, because, at best it's a short-term fix. You'll need a strong emotional bond to have good sex, let alone TBSI, no matter how much Viagra or estrogen you take. Your sexuality has changed, in terms of your ability to perform at your peak absent an emotional component, and you can either embrace a new sexual paradigm or watch your sex life go into precipitous decline. A strong emotional connection is an absolute if boomers want to enjoy TBSI for decades to come.

Get In Shape

To engage in TBSI, you'll need to get into some semblance of physical condition. If you couldn't think of a reason to do this in the past, perhaps the promise that TBSI delivers will give you that incentive. TBSI is sometimes aerobic, which means that besides feeling incredibly good, it's also good for you. But you aren't going to be up to aerobic sex if you're lugging around a big belly. You don't need to consult a chart to know if you're overweight. The test for men is simple. Get naked, stand up straight, and look down. If all you can see is the floor, you're not in shape for any kind of sex, and in fact may be putting yourself at a health risk. If you can see your toes you're approaching a good sexual plateau, and if you can see your feet, you're totally ready for TBSI.

There was an ambulance parked outside my gym the last two times I worked out. Both times the paramedics were loading older, overweight guys onto gurneys because they'd overdone their workouts. These men had passed out, and while neither man died or was in serious condition, this is avoidable. If you're out of shape and want to get into shape to enjoy sex more or just to feel good, talk to your doctor first and take it slow. That belly you've developed over time isn't just a few sit-ups away from disappearing, so give yourself at least a few months to allow your body to get into the rhythm of exercising before becoming sexually aggressive.

The treadmill is a good start; slow and easy for half an hour without any incline is smart. As your heart develops the ability to handle your exercise program you can amp it up accordingly. If you combine this with a diet high in fruits, vegetables, and whole grains, the weight will drop off rapidly.

On a personal level, I'm not a fitness fanatic but I work out at the gym four or five times a week. I also watch how much and what I eat. I advocate getting into shape to improve the quality of your sex life, but of course there are lots of other health benefits.

I've never met a woman who enjoyed sex while pinned down by a big belly. The handful of times I couldn't perform sexually was with very overweight women. Unless you're willing to make doggy-style the only possible sexual position because of your girth, I can't imagine a better reason to get fit. If you can't decide if it's worth the effort, you may not be ready for TBSI, but until you've experienced it, you really don't know what you're missing. There's a sexual lethargy that is part of being overweight that holds boomer men and women back, and doesn't allow for sweet physical intimacy. Sex is one of your basic needs, and since it's so pleasurable, getting into better shape seems like a small price to enjoy it fully. You'll like how you look and feel too, and so will your partner.

Food, The Best Sex Imaginable, and The 5 Senses

My love for sex and food are nearly equal. Both involve the senses, and while no one needs to be reminded that appreciating good food involves sight, taste, touch, and smell, great sex requires all of those, plus hearing. TBSI is a 5-pronged sensual experience.

Sight

Every man and woman wants to feel special to his or her partner, and a major part of that special feeling is how desirable our partner makes us feel by the way they look at us. It's the most obvious sexual turn on. It's so powerful in fact, that just watching my partner walk across the room naked arouses me. Joe Cocker said it perfectly in his 1974 hit, "You Are So Beautiful," to which he added the most important two words, "to me." My visual stimulation is due in great part to our emotional connection, because how I feel about her influences how I see her. I adore her, so when we get together after being apart even briefly, I see a beautiful, sensual woman who I know loves me and can't wait to make love to me. This is how it's supposed to feel incidentally, and while it's typically about the newness at first, it develops well beyond that with the growing depth of feeling for each other.

When I was actively dating, I relied primarily on my sense of sight to determine whether a woman interested me sexually, usually from the photos she posted on her online dating profile. Her physical attraction was important to me. But I wasn't looking for Hollywood's version of beautiful, and preferred an authentic smile, which indicated a joyful woman. It's difficult to imagine being in a fun-filled relationship with a depressed or sad man or woman. While this may seem unfair, a man or woman who can't conjure up a smile for a photo he or she knows everyone will see, will probably find it difficult to smile in person, too.

If I felt a spark from a profile, and was encouraged by an email response, I followed up with a phone call before I met a woman for coffee, because voice is important too. I always showed up for a coffee date at the café a few minutes early so I could watch a woman walk to my table. It's the way she looked of course, but also the way she moved, that peaked my interest. I looked for the inner beauty that lives just under the surface, which I noticed in her smile and her eyes, both of which suggest warmth. A woman who smiled when we said hello was automatically attractive, and I felt delighted to meet her, no matter what followed.

While I appreciate the feminine form, my admiration isn't related to perfection. We're boomers, and we're not as firm or perfect as we may have once been; a few pounds and wrinkles are symbols of aging that I can easily overlook. Having said this, it's still important to be able to see the other person's body as beautiful if you hope to enjoy that person fully, which has nothing to do with perfection, and everything to do with personal taste, and hopefully a strong emotional connection.

Staring into each other's eyes while kissing deeply is red hot when partners are emotionally connected. Movie actors often close their eyes while kissing, but I suggest that's a mistake in real life, because you'll miss seeing something special. Gaze into your partner's eyes while making love and you'll actually be able to see the love; seeing this in your sweetheart's eyes will enhance your desire. You may never have actually seen love in such a powerful way before.

Looking at my partner's body, which isn't perfect, makes me crazy with desire. I've fallen so deeply in love with her and the way she looks at me, that just watching her sleep next to me fills me with desire. It's important to look deeper than the surface. When boomer men or women mention dating younger people, it suggests they require physical perfection to become aroused. This is when an emotional connection matters most, because feelings trump imperfections.

Here's the bottom line for boomers who feel they need young partners to become aroused. Whatever it is that makes you hot looking at a young man or woman isn't going to sustain your performance for long, and ultimately you're going to end up back where you started, needing something new to become aroused. This is counterproductive, because you'll discover that the fountain of youth effect with young men and women has a short shelf life.

Get comfortable with your aging body, and you'll be able to admire the boomer man or woman living happily in theirs. It's easy to fall in love with a man or woman you can resonate with on every level.

Touch

Touch is a sense we're anxious to use when we see our partner, whether naked or clothed. Holding your partner in your arms should be an irresistible urge. Your desire to touch and hold each other should feel automatic. Sexual touching is ritualistic, primitive, and a major contributor to TBSI. Don't settle for less. Touch is too important to skip.

Squeezing a woman's breasts or stroking a man like a pull toy isn't foreplay. A woman's breasts consist of more than her nipples, and a man's peter is actually fairly fragile. Other parts of our bodies are also erotic and crave attention. The soft, tender, flesh between a woman's thighs is heavenly to caress, tease, and kiss lightly, as is her lower back and of course, her kitty. Kissing and touching these spots gently while inhaling the blend of her body's natural aromas can make both partners wild with desire. Many guys are fans of a woman's derriere; its essential nature is also arousing.

A man's erotic zone is more than just his peter. Cupping a man's balls gently and rolling them in your hands and mouth will put a man on the road to TBSI. The soft spot under his balls also reacts to touch and when a woman ventures there a man becomes sexually charged.

No Limits

Simply put, there's nothing sexual that's off limits, so don't deprive yourself of any pleasure. A big part of TBSI is both partners allowing themselves to feel out of control with desire, completely vulnerable and giving, as well as feeling addicted to each other's bodies because you love each other deeply. Since TBSI is about two people loving and adoring each other, the quality of it actually increases as that connection deepens.

Deep kissing as well as orally pleasuring each other adds another layer of enjoyment, because you and your partner can taste and smell the intimacy on each other's lips. This is something sweet to share. Afterward, you may want to think of intercourse in terms of a waltz rather than a steam piston. That slow dance can last an entire evening, because you can rest, hug, and stare into each other's eyes, until you're both ready to continue.

Piston-like pounding isn't necessarily your best option for many reasons, not the least of which is stamina for men, and pain for women. Boomers can easily learn to become slow dancers and appreciate the longer-lasting pleasure of a sexual waltz. There's no hurry since sex isn't something to get out of the way. TBSI produces orgasms for you and your partner that can take the two of you to another planet, multiple times, and boomer men can orgasm repeatedly without ejaculating, one of the advantages of getting older. Basically, boomer men can last almost as long as they want, and longer if they're fit.

Assuming there's a deep, loving connection, TBSI can begin as quickly as a couple feel safe enough to move beyond previously held sexual inhibitions. Explore each other's bodies with abandon is what foreplay is meant to produce, and it shouldn't be shortchanged. TBSI occurs when partners move beyond the limitations that render sex uninspired, kind of like cooking without salt even when salt is available.

Sound

Nothing is more exciting than hearing your partner pant and moan with desire, knowing that he or she is aroused. Enjoy talking while making love, since most men and women appreciate it. Talking trash, or telling your partner how much you love them, is infinitely more sensual than silence, which is not necessarily golden during sex. In fact, silence can be awkward and boring. Give your inhibitions a rest and stop thinking when making love. Allow your inner sexual self to rise to the surface and express your feelings in the moment.

My partner began whispering my name repeatedly while making love one evening, and that took me to a higher sexual plateau. No one had done that before, and the more she whispered my name the better sex felt. Repeating my name made sex more personal, and since it was new to me, I felt like I was her first lover, a sweet fantasy. When my partner responds in kind to my sexual banter I know she's thoroughly engaged.

Since I love talking during sex, and my partner enjoys it too, what we say to each other isn't scripted. Sometimes it's romantic and loving, and other times it's profane. It's whatever turns us on in that moment, but there aren't any bad choices. It's a sweet form of eroticism. You can talk your partner into and through an orgasm, because you know what he or she likes to hear while you're making love. Being verbal and noisy is a natural aspect of being sexual, and absent dialogue, sex may lack some of the fun factor that playful banter produces. Nothing that couples say to each other is wrong as long as it turns both partners on. If you don't know where or how to begin simply tell your partner how sex is feeling for you in the moment, as colorfully as you can imagine. In a short while you'll be writing your own sexual script that will hopefully never be finished.

Taste

No food ever tasted or smelled as sweet as a woman's body to me, and not just her kitty, although that's intoxicating and makes me hungry with desire. Boomer women's kitties are less musky than younger women's and have a subtle aroma that's uniquely wonderful. I thoroughly enjoy the taste of my partner, which is sweeter than a dessert wine.

If you're a guy who'd rather watch sports on television than have sex with a willing, loving partner, you might want to have your testosterone level checked or rethink your recreational priorities, because TBSI with someone special is so unique that the joy can't be duplicated in any other arena, especially not on television.

Sex is a gift waiting to be unwrapped and enjoyed. Watching television can never be as good. What do you suppose the guys playing sports on television would rather be doing? Considering the copious amount of press devoted to the sexual adventures of professional athletes off the field, sex is likely at the top of their list of choices. Record the game and watch it later in bed, holding your sweetie in your arms while she sleeps. That's a win/win.

Smell

There's much more than the taste of my partner's kitty. I bury my face in her armpits and inhale her like it's pure oxygen. It's an aroma I never miss. After the sweat begins to flow, the earthiness and pungency of that aroma gets even better. We don't use deodorant when we know we're going to be intimate, because it prevents exactly what we want, which is being able to enjoy each other's natural essences. Forget advertisements for products whose purpose is to mask these natural essences, light perfume excepted because it mixes well with sweat.

My partner's derriere is a favorite. It's basic and earthy. Forget about preconceived notions of right and wrong, clean and dirty, or whatever anyone ever told you was sexually appropriate, because everything in sex is appropriate. In combination with her kitty and armpits, it's the trifecta of sexual olfactory arousal. Don't ignore any of these because of foolish old taboos. Get TBSI wild.

My partner eagerly inhales my chest, neck, hair, peter, balls and more, driving me equally wild. Sweat doesn't preclude any of this and. in fact, it adds to the sexual soup. Once a man or woman becomes intoxicated with these aromas, intercourse enters a different dimension, the TBSI zone, apologies to Rod Serling. To become TBSI aroused, the sense of smell is critical. Inhaling my partner makes me feel hotter than I did as a younger man, before I appreciated enjoying a woman's entire body. But still, it's our emotional connection that allows us to reach greater heights. Absent all 5 senses, sex is like a cake that's not fully baked.

Sex or Food?

It depends on what kind of hungry you're feeling, but they can also be enjoyed together. Feeding each other what I think of in terms of love food, i.e. strawberries, chocolates, cut-up fruit, etc. in bed after making love is a joyful way to extend the playfulness and pleasure while laying together on a blissful cloud. Messy? Sure, but great sex isn't meant to be neat and tidy. I enjoy bringing my partner breakfast in bed on the weekends after we make love. I'm suggesting coffee and cut up fruit and maybe a slice of toast or a muffin, not the Lumberjack Slam Breakfast at Denny's. Think light. The idea is to slake your hunger and feed your senses, but leave room for dessert, more cuddling and sex.

Sexually Overactive?

I'm thrilled to be a sexually active 69 year-old man in a perpetually hot sexual relationship with a 65 year-old woman. Getting older has nothing to do with enjoying sex at the highest and most enjoyable level. While this isn't any boomer's first rodeo, anyone who thinks a boomer's best sexual years are behind them isn't having TBSI.

What's more pleasurable than sex? Reading, watching a movie, cooking, hiking, art museums, the ballet, and riding motorcycles, are all first class entertainment, but none feels as satisfying as sex with my partner.

Loving, passionate, uninhibited sex is a wonderful gift from whatever god you hold in your heart. It was men, for self-serving reasons, that invented the notion that this gift comes with rules. Loving sex is a powerful bonding experience that's both physically and emotionally healthy. Which begs the question of why, since we're such a sex-obsessed nation, aren't we having more sex? Perhaps the plethora of porn has dulled our sexual senses and appetites, especially since love isn't something porn ever suggests. I've read that the average sexual tryst between lovers is seven minutes. That seems woefully short to me, and that briefness reflects porn in terms of getting on and getting off as quickly as possible. Give porn a rest and become sensitized to sex again in a healthy manner. I know with certainty that more love translates into more sex and that this requires letting go of fear around showing and talking about your feelings with your partner.

Peters and Kitties

If you're a recently single boomer guy, like most men you wake up with an erection every morning, and you're probably chomping at the bit for your first, post-breakup sexual adventure. Your morning erection gives you some amount of confidence about your lovemaking capabilities. Unfortunately, it's not always that simple. What you may not have factored in is, as I've mentioned, is that boomer guys perform best when there's an emotional connection with their partners. Performance anxiety can wilt the best of men's intentions, but it's avoidable. Feeling deeply in love and having that level of love returned absolutely increases sexual potency. And, of course it also increases the level of pleasure.

If you're a woman, your concerns may be somewhat different. Can you become aroused in the manner you did decades ago? You may also be worried about pain, since you may not have been sexual in a while, and your physicality has changed. Perhaps you're not sure you'll still enjoy sex, and you already know that casual sex won't work for you. You've talked with your boomer women friends and discovered that many are still enjoying TBSI with their long-term partners. No reasons to worry to the point of distraction or omission.

Investing Your Heart

Single boomer women quickly discover that their women friends still having TBSI, share certain factors in common in their relationships, but the most important is that they're with men who love them on a deep level, and are patient and considerate lovers. They're still in love with their men, and they're also focused on being good lovers. I'm positive there's a powerful heart connection that's contributing heavily to their terrific sex lives. The passion and love they feel for each other continues to grow.

The Best Sex Imaginable Begins in the Heart

I've never talked about sex with any boomer guy who insisted he was having great sex with a partner who wasn't totally accommodating in bed. Of course, the same is also true for women. In addition, the more powerful the emotional connection between them, the better the sex. Boomers can't depend solely on their bodies to perform at their sexual peak like they could decades ago. For boomers, TBSI rests heavily on this emotional connection.

But, don't panic guys; it's simple, really. It's important that men recognize there's nothing unmanly about sharing their feelings with women. On the contrary, it's the epitome of masculinity for a man to be able to express his feelings to a woman. I assure every man that few women will ever confuse your ability to express your feelings for weakness.

Bridging the gap between nervous men and women who want to be sexual after long dry spells is the first step. It's a mutual understanding of what works for each other within a loving, committed relationship that creates TBSI, and that may not look the same for everyone. Having said this there seem to be some universal sexual truths.

The Rules

The first rule for creating TBSI is that there are no rules, in terms of what's appropriate and what isn't. Yeah, I know, everyone says that, and then they add, as long as both people are in agreement. I'm expanding on this by including an appreciation for each other's bodies on a level some boomers haven't considered or experienced. Thinking outside of the sexual box may not come easily, no pun intended, since old habits die hard, but there's a blissful pot of gold at the end of this rainbow. More couples might use their sexual potential, more fully. And this shouldn't be limited in any way because we're older, and some of us aren't as agile as we once were. Everything I've mentioned can be enjoyed to whatever degree is physically possible. While I feel the better shape we're in, the better the sexual experience, that doesn't preclude anyone not in tiptop shape, or with some disabilities, from fully enjoying sex.

Embrace Imperfection

There are lots of reasons and excuses why more boomers aren't having more sex, and in particular, imperfect, aging bodies, are frequently mentioned as diminishing sexual desire. A few extra pounds, stretch marks, wrinkles, etc. get paid considerable attention, while looking into each other's eyes where the love is noticeable, doesn't get nearly enough.

While I previously mentioned that it's imperative to find a partner who's your physical fantasy, that doesn't mean that only perfect bodies make the cut. Seeing beyond imperfection has a lot to do with how a man and a woman feel about each other. On that basis, any imperfections become less noticeable and less important. It's sad and wrong-headed how boomer women are made to feel old and ugly by a media that's skull locked on twenty-year old women's tight bodies. A man who adopts this flawed media standard is a victim of the media, and he isn't likely find love with a twenty-year old woman, or any woman for that matter.

The standard for men is also unrealistic. It's improbable that many boomer men could be body doubles for George Clooney, but men don't need to feel less attractive because they can't. The easiest way for boomer men to look youthful and handsome is to just to be in reasonably good shape. That doesn't mean six-pack abs, but it also doesn't mean sporting a belly hanging over your belt buckle.

My partner is in great shape for a woman in her mid-sixties, but gravity has taken its toll. Her breasts are beautiful to me, perkiness notwithstanding, and the rest of her body is as beautiful to me as if she were decades younger. Fantasy and imperfection are not mutually exclusive.

Some boomers suffer from physical issues that may preclude the sexual positions and acrobatics of their youths, but that still leaves ample room to enjoy TBSI, since it begins with a heart connection anyway. I don't want to suggest that perfection is necessary, in terms of being capable of sex, and there are many ways to circumvent physical issues.

Your Heart is More Than a Pump

If boomer men hope to maintain a high level of sexuality, they're going to have to engage their entire personas, including their hearts. The flip side to casual sex becoming less viable for most boomer men is that the older men become, the longer we're able to perform, since we no longer ejaculate as quickly. Men can also have multiple orgasms when they don't ejaculate, and that makes boomer men very potent guys. What I've discovered to be universally true, is that the more love we feel for our partners, the more sexual energy we have. In fact, assuming men are in reasonably good shape, we can make love for hours. If you have to ask why a man would want to make love for hours, you haven't had TBSI. Viagra or Cialis work of course, but they work far better in tandem with a loving heart. Since ED pills don't get you up, but rather keep you up, it's the love in your heart that accomplishes the former.

Sex feels so good to most men that we never want it to end, period. And ejaculating is rarely the goal since it signifies the end of making love, which boomer men can avoid for as long as they want. If you haven't made extended love in a while, or ever, you're cheating yourself out of a terrific experience. The reason engaging hearts was less important when we were younger, was that our bodies could manage without much or even any emotional stimulation. That's no longer true as men age.

Sexual Delusions

While boomer men blissfully fill Viagra prescriptions and fantasize about being stallions again, and boomer women use hormones and estrogen rings, remembering how quickly we used to become aroused, the pressure to actually have sex builds like steam in a kettle. The expectation level can become so unrealistically high, that dysfunction and disappointment are inevitable. No amount of Viagra will enable a man to perform at his peak without an emotional connection. So how can boomer men and women embrace each other's hearts and end up wearing post-sexual tryst smiles?

Ask For What You Want

Before going off on a tangent about connecting hearts with TBSI, some honesty and clarity about flawed notions of sexuality is warranted. It amazes me that couples can be together for years without ever telling each other what they want or like, sexually. Whether this holding back of critical information is due to shyness, inexperience, fear, lack of knowledge, or inhibitions, the result is the same; sexual frustration, usually followed by resentment.

When a man or woman insist that they cheat on their partner because they can't get what they want in bed, I suspect it's either because they haven't asked for what they want, or they're with the wrong lover. I remember Woody Allen's interview on The Tonight Show many years ago. Johnny Carson asked him if he thought sex was dirty. Woody's response was spot on, "Only if it's done right." Uninhibited is a better descriptive word than dirty. It isn't selfish to tell your partner what you want, and unless it's something that's going to cause pain, it shouldn't be a problem either. Pleasing a partner should be enjoyable, and denying your partner any pleasure he or she enjoys is wrong-headed.

Cleanliness Isn't Always Next to Godliness

Unless you're restricted by some unfortunate, misguided, moral or religious positions about sex, you should know that sex of the TBSI variety is totally uninhibited. It relies on love, which everyone can agree is important in a relationship, but is critical for great sex. Women have shared their sexual histories with me over the years, and I've been surprised to learn some men have issues about a woman's hygiene before sex. Some even insist a woman take a bath first, which seems counterintuitive since I've always felt the opposite is desirable for women to preserve their natural aromas.

If the taste and aroma of a woman's kitty in its natural state doesn't seem right to you, you're missing out on a major aspect of her sexuality and your own pleasure too. Why would soap or douche taste or smell better than a woman's natural aroma? Since boomer women have a subtle aroma after menopause, even the most olfactory sensitive men should feel comfortable. Hang-ups regarding hygiene and sex deserve consideration, because misleading douche advertisements have poisoned the well. The notion that a woman's entire body is anything but perfect in its natural state, is a hoax perpetrated for profit.

What's Good for the Goose

The same principle applies to women regarding sex with men. The reasons why a woman would eschew being oral with a man don't come from an emotionally healthy place. Someone had to put the idea into a woman's head that performing oral sex on a man is wrong. TBSI will never become a reality for men and women until they eliminate their sexual hang-ups. Oral sex is an intimate act, in terms of tasting your partner's sexuality, and making love with your lips and tongue. Nothing two people in love do together, sexually, is ever wrong.

Be Specific Making Sexual Requests

The only sexual rule that matters is doing whatever makes both people as wild about being sexual together as possible. What does that mean? It means if you'd like a woman to fondle your balls when she's sucking your peter you're going to have to tell her that's what you want. She isn't going to know what drives you wild if you don't, since whatever that is, is unique to each person. If you're a woman who enjoys a man gently rubbing soft, slow circles on your G spot while licking your clitoris, you're going to have to tell him. Whether it's a finger, a tongue, or whatever makes you crazy with desire, it's absolutely okay. The word *perversion* should be eliminated from the sexual lexicon, because it suggests there's a right and wrong regarding sex, and there are no wrongs in TBSI, since both partners love each other.

God Yes, Guilt No

While the missionary position works fine, the name alone might give you pause, regarding whether it's the only or best way to have sex. I don't believe sex is connected to religion unless you subscribe to the notion that sex is only meant to procreate. Since a boomer woman can no longer procreate, that would mean that her sex life is over after menopause, which for many women begins around forty. No one has the right to suggest something that stern and disrespectful. Religious zealots and moral policemen frequently oppose human pleasure, sex included, and they do so in the name of a higher authority. They should be ignored because I believe everyone's god loves them and wants them to enjoy everything in life, including sex, and especially when it's an expression of love.

C'mon Doc

It would seem that some experts who write about sex still haven't had their first blowjob. I remember reading *Everything You Ever Wanted to Know About Sex,* many years ago. The author, Dr. David Reuben, wrote that he honestly couldn't understand why men were so fascinated with getting their penises sucked. Really Doc? You really can't understand why? Okay, maybe you don't, but your confusion is a poor reason to suggest there's something wrong with a man who loves fellatio. Sexual ignorance is not bliss, and worse, it puts sexual bliss out of reach. Anyone who espouses anything that limits sexual enjoyment needs to look into a mirror and figure out how he or she became so wrong-headed about one of the few things in life that doesn't need any rules. Hypocrites and fools abound when sex is the topic, and considering the number of sexual scandals involving moral hypocrites, perhaps everyone should just mind his or her own business.

Anatomy 101

Boomer men might brush up on women's anatomy, especially if foreplay hasn't ever been a major part of their sexuality. Foreplay is important and it is every bit as exciting, and nearly as satisfying as intercourse; avoiding or rushing it is shortsighted and selfish. A woman's body is complex, and paying attention to it on a detailed level, is helpful to satisfy her. She's a boomer, and while this isn't her first rodeo, and she may not know all of the things that work for her, she absolutely knows the things that don't. Ask her what she likes instead of deciding for her. You may be surprised by what she wants, but you love her, so pleasing her should be your only priority. It's a couple's willingness to explore their relationship's sexuality that keeps it fresh and exciting.

Sexual Attitudes

How a sexual request is made is equally important as the request itself, because if it's made in a judgmental manner i.e., "Why don't you ever," (fill in the blank), the other person will be defending him or herself instead of listening. Drop any preconceived notions of good and bad, or right and wrong, and ask what your partner would like instead. Be open to hearing things that may surprise you even after being with someone for a while. And be grateful your partner had the courage to ask you to fulfill his or her fantasies. This is a critical step towards enjoying sexual bliss together and deepening the relationship connection, so don't let your ego get in the way. Deliver the goods enthusiastically and unselfishly. Assuming you're with someone who truly loves you, you needn't worry about him or her responding in kind, because they'll be delighted to. TBSI is always mutually satisfying.

One of the most exciting aspects of boomer sex is the promise that increased information holds toward creating better sex. The number of women who rarely, if ever, had orgasms with their ex's is surprising. A couple of minutes of fondling a woman aren't going to get her to the finish line. A man whose marriage didn't include oral sex, even though he desperately wanted it, isn't going to be satisfied with a hand job. Focus all of your energy and attention on pleasing your partner, instead of wondering if he or she is going to give you what you want in return. Your mutual desire to pleasure each other is simpler than focusing on your own needs. Relax and make love like you're in a sexual fantasy theme park. Since it's all about love, everything a man and woman do together sexually is perfect.

What Kind of Sex Partner Are You?

This is critical since it indicates your willingness to please your partner in his or her unique way. A totally willing and giving sex partner is the gold standard, and moving beyond self-imposed limitations is the easiest way to attain that standard. If a man or woman wants to experience a level of pleasure they previously haven't, opening their hearts to match their desires can make the difference. Since you have enormous love in your heart for your partner, absolutely nothing that pleases him or her should feel out of bounds. Honor his or her requests gladly.

Finding the Right Sexual Partner

Finding TBSI partner that will light you up like a Christmas tree isn't as simple as just physical attraction, although that matters too. It's also about matching sexual attitudes. TBSI occurs when two people in love who are physically attracted to each other have nearly identical sexual proclivities, and feel open about sharing them with each other.

You can't tell whether or not someone is inhibited simply by his or her looks. Sometimes the least inhibited person looks like what you imagine the most inhibited might. This is definitely a case for not judging a book by its cover. I've dated beautiful, sensual women who had so many sexual hang-ups that sex was awful, and I've heard women's stories about handsome, in shape guys whose notion of good sex was climbing on, getting off, and falling asleep. This isn't a conversation best had over a coffee date, but rather one to be had after both partners agree that they're ready to be sexual.

I've been with women who've told me, "You can do whatever you want to me," but it was usually about a desire to be physically used and abused, and had little to do with trusting or loving me. For some, this may pass for love but, after experiencing it, I have a different take. Love has nothing to do with it. My partner said this to me shortly after we became sexual, and it was entirely about trust. I wouldn't dream of causing her pain or abusing her in any way, but knowing that she loves and trusts me enough to be completely sexually open, excites me. It also allows me to inject new sexual ideas into our relationship. A woman, who tells me that I can do whatever I want to her because she loves and trusts me, makes me feel powerful, and also encourages me to please her.

This isn't a topic that couples should wait patiently to bring up either. It's too important for that. Once the decision to become sexual is agreed on, that's the time for sharing sexual truths. The simplest way to ease into this discussion is to begin with the premise that nothing sexual is off-limits and see where that takes the conversation. Will it kill the moment? No, but more important than that moment is what your sex life is going to look like with that person for years to come. If you're a man or woman whose marriage didn't include the sexual playfulness you craved, for heaven's sake, don't repeat that mistake no matter the other qualities your current partner has. Great sex is your right, period.

Bad Sex Rarely Gets Better

Here's what I know to be true for nearly every man or woman with whom I've ever had a sexual conversation. When a sexual relationship with a man or woman was hot right from the start, it typically got hotter as they fell deeper in love. When sex was marginal, clumsy, and unfulfilling in the beginning, it rarely got better enough. Sometimes, even when two people feel they're in love, they don't fit together sexually. This is about chemistry and attitude. Don't settle because you'll waste too much time wondering why you got sucked into another relationship that lacked sexual heat. If you think money, status, compatibility, or power, are substitutes for great sex, think again.

Cheating

I'm not going to spend a lot of space addressing infidelity because there are reasons for it other than lack of sex. You deserve to have every one of your sexual fantasies become realities, and you shouldn't have to cheat to make that happen. At a minimum, discussing the sexual nature of your relationship is a worthwhile conversation, and since it's possible to improve the quality of the sexual connection in your relationship if love still exists, it may be productive as well. Having said this, I would never suggest a man or woman remain in a relationship that lacks the sexual pleasures they fantasize about. Life is too short for that.

Sexual Heat

Is sexual heat important for everyone? When I hear someone say that their relationship doesn't include great sex, but that they remain in it because it has many other good qualities, I cringe, because the truth for all but a few, is that great sex is a major factor in a great relationship. If you're in a relationship now in which sex is an afterthought or a struggle between your desires and the other person's limitations, maybe it's time to re-evaluate. It annoys me when I hear someone say that sex isn't all that important in boomer relationships. Maybe for that person it isn't; and anyone who dates that person has a right to know that sex isn't the bomb for him or her before they consider starting a relationship. For boomers deeply in love, TBSI shouldn't be skipped.

How Long Is Sex Supposed to Last?

This is really simple. Sex should last as long as you and your partner can make it last and still enjoy it. Taking sexual enhancement pills to extend sexual play, beyond what you can manage on your own, makes perfect sense as long as your partner is in sync with your desires. Why would anyone want to make love all night long? You're joking, right? It feels so good that I can't imagine why anyone would ever want it to end, because it embodies the love you and your partner feel for each other.

Even after lengthy foreplay and intercourse, alternating back and forth to rest a bit, sex doesn't have to end. Waking up and making love in the morning is a wonderful way to start your day, as is spending part of the weekend in bed, making love, taking naps, eating, talking, reading, and just relaxing together. TBSI is that good, so don't cheat yourself by thinking in terms of a quickie. Great sex isn't a snack. If you and your partner haven't spent a weekend in bed, consider what's preventing it. I don't mean every weekend or all weekend long, but make a date at least on a once in a while basis. If you feel that going to the mall is more pleasurable than sex, perhaps you need to talk about the sexual nature of your relationship, and rekindle the spark that was once there.

There are lots of variations on the theme, and they're all cool, because great sex is whatever works for two people deeply in love, and not what anyone says should be acceptable. Soft, hard, dominant, submissive, and any other variations of sexual play are terrific as long as both partners are in sync. And, if they can't agree, perhaps their sexual relationship needs a re-evaluation, because this is too important to relegate to the back seat of a relationship. Great sex, unlike great food, isn't fattening, doesn't require a trip to the market, has no cooking/waiting time, and is equally tasty.

Sexual Dominance

I'm sexually dominant like the majority of men, so the notion of being submissive feels wrong since it goes against everything I consider sexually exciting. That doesn't mean I should learn to be submissive either because sexual preferences are, for the most part, second nature. Of course, the opposite for other couples may be true. My partner is a submissive woman and she enjoys being sexually dominated. We know what we like sexually and we share that information with each other openly, since we both love sex and want ours to remain the best possible. Sex has to be the most universal recreational activity in the world and I remember reading that tens of millions of people are making love at any given time, day or night. But in terms of what works for everyone on an individual basis, there is no universal. There is no good or bad, right or wrong, sexually. There is only what brings couples in love, the maximum pleasure.

Dominant Sex

Using "dominant" to describe a sexual preference refers to being sexually in command of your partner. This has nothing whatsoever to do with other aspects of your partner's life. My partner is a fully empowered woman with a successful career and loads of accomplishments and great self-esteem. That she likes to be dominated in bed is independent of how she expects to be treated out of bed. I wouldn't dream of trying to dominate her in any other way, and, frankly I wouldn't enjoy that anyway.

Many, if not most, couples practice Tarzan and Jane sex in bed, and it usually works so well that neither partner would dream of changing it. Partners often assume entirely different personas in bed, and a man or woman who captains their sex life does so with respect. It's about sexual power and dominance, not pain. Being sexually dominant doesn't mean your partner's pleasure isn't tantamount. That both partners have orgasms during sex should encourage them to continue performing well.

Practice Makes Perfect

Ideally a couple's sexual skills become mutually practiced, to the point that they no longer require prompting or instruction. The tastes and aromas of each other's bodies are intoxicating when appreciated in the context of love. Worshiping and pleasuring each other without a scintilla of inhibition or sense of right or wrong is key. If boomer sex isn't about maximizing pleasure for the partner you love, then what is it about?

Kissing

TBSI begins with kissing. Pretty basic stuff, but if you have some phobias around kissing it's way past the time to move beyond them. If you have hygiene issues, suggest brushing or flossing before kissing. Whatever it takes to get you locking lips is okay.

Looking into each other's eyes while kissing adds another dimension to sex. Yeah, I know, it's a no brainer, right? Wrong. How many partners have told you what a great kisser you are? When I gaze into my partner's eyes, they tell me the absolute truth, and the way she looks into my eyes turns me on even more than when she tells me show loves me.

If TBSI is your goal, kissing should be passionate and without any time considerations. Sucking on each other's lips is wonderfully erotic. How much kissing is appropriate before intercourse? As much kissing as it takes for both partners to feel ready for the main event. I can kiss my partner for a long while before moving on to other types of foreplay, but the more we kiss the hotter we feel for each other.

Boomer Men Need Foreplay Too

Incidentally, the notion that boomer women require more foreplay than men simply isn't true. Both need as much foreplay as possible for peak performance. Sure, men often become erect quickly, but that doesn't mean they're necessarily ready for TBSI; losing an erection because you weren't sufficiently aroused is unnecessary. There's a Tantric practice that teaches men how to orgasm without ejaculating. But this is something older guys can do naturally since ejaculating becomes more difficult and less frequent as we age, while having orgasms doesn't. This is great news because it affords men the ability to orgasm repeatedly since ejaculation is delayed. I've had as many as a half dozen orgasms in an evening, and friends have reported similar results. When that occurs, making love the next morning can be even sweeter because that's when a man can allow himself to ejaculate. What a perfect way to begin the day.

A Note of Caution

The number of boomers becoming infected with sexually transmitted diseases is shockingly high, and, worse, it's climbing. While I don't advocate casual sex, it's not for moral reasons, but rather the quality of the sexual experience. Casual sex demands the use of condoms, and the notion that boomers are old enough to know better doesn't seem to be true considering the statistics. Using condoms is an absolute must unless, or until, both partners have been tested. Condoms were never our generation's favorite method of contraception, but the odds of becoming infected with an STD overrides choice.

Condoms can be made a part of sexual play with a little imagination. A woman putting a condom on a man can be very sensual, especially if she's somewhat skilled. No matter how much fun condoms may or may not be, they shouldn't ever be considered optional in a relationship until a couple gets tested. Enjoy TBSI with your new partner, but please play safe until you know it is okay to have unprotected sex. Your health, and maybe even your life depend on it.

Chapter Eleven:
What's Next?

The Finish Line

The ultimate goal for most dating boomers is to go on their last, first date, which would mean they've met their one true love, the man or woman that makes them feel their search has unquestionably ended. Identifying your life partner involves the ability to weigh his or her physical and emotional health to a reasonably satisfying conclusion, and the goal is that both are as nearly perfect as possible. This isn't easily quantifiable, but suffice to say the relevance of a person's physical and emotional health can't be ignored no matter their other attributes. We all want to be in a relationship that nourishes our spirit, and not one that drains it. On a personal level, it took what felt like forever to finally meet my partner nearly two years ago, and in the years I previously spent searching for her what kept me going was that I never lost sight of the fact that she was out there looking for me too. We're currently in the period of deciding what's next, so this chapter is personal and hopefully informative too.

Finding Mr. or Mrs. Right is Just the Beginning

Okay, you think you've found the nearly perfect man or woman after dating for a while. So what's next? Before you decide, take a step back for a moment. It's critical to examine your relationship from every standpoint regarding all of the components that successful relationships share in common. A few issues immediately come to mind. Does your relationship include an emotional connection that when tested under duress has proven resilient? Do you and your partner effectively resolve issues that arise through emotionally honest dialogue, or do problems become circular arguments that don't resolve anything, and pop up over and over again? Is the sexual aspect of your relationship as passionate and exciting as you hoped it would be? Do you and your partner discuss the sexual nature and quality of your relationship with the goal of improving it? Are your sexual fantasies becoming your realities? Is your partner also your best friend? Is trust the glue that binds your relationship together? These are critical long-term relationship qualities that can't be ignored. All successful boomer relationship partners can answer yes to each question.

Okay, your relationship has passed the first test. There are several possibilities in terms of where it might go next—and the outcome is for the two of you to determine by using all the emotional honesty and clarity you've learned to muster in your relationship. What's next is a decision for the two of you to make on your own timetable. This is not a decision that necessarily benefits from polling friends and relatives. We're seasoned boomers, and while we're hoping our next relationship will be our last, listening to other people's doubts and opinions can just muddy the waters.

Having said that, there are harmful issues that can't ever be ignored, such as substance abuse or unresolved mental health issues. A friend, who's willing to risk his or her friendship with you, by pointing out either of these issues if they notice they're present in your partner, is a best friend. Sometimes in our moments of need and optimistic joy we may ignore a partner's detrimental issues, because we're so eager to be in a relationship that we become blind to the truth. In those muddled moments, it's hard to walk the line separating candor and intrusiveness with an open and honest friend. A friend's concern regarding substance abuse or serious mental health issues is a wake-up call you want to heed.

Making Choices

There are several paths couples can take after both partners feel their relationship has withstood at least some test of time, and have answered the questions posed. How much time depends entirely on what each couple feels is appropriate, and there are no hard and fast rules. Having said that however, a few months aren't typically enough to make an informed decision. The decision to take a relationship to the next level after falling in love and building a solid relationship foundation requires quite a lot of dialogue and consideration. We're boomers, we've all made relationship mistakes, and we all want to get it right this time. Cautious optimism is a helpful attitude.

The reality is that there aren't that many choices, so the possibilities may seem limited. Making the best one is complicated, so rushing in any direction is a mistake. Couples may continue to date casually but not exclusively, date exclusively and perhaps spend weekends together, live together, part or full time, or get married. These are the most commonly chosen paths.

Your Past Catches Up With You

For many boomers, and particularly boomers that have been in several long-term relationships, choosing to continue dating may feel like the most comfortable path since it's less demanding and restrictive than cohabitation or marriage. Remembering the sting that may have felt like a lack of freedom in a past relationship, particularly one with control issues can cloud making the best decision. While no one wants to experience another failed relationship, no one wants to miss a golden opportunity for a successful one either.

Feeling claustrophobic in a past relationship certainly isn't going to make a person feel warm and fuzzy about taking a relationship deeper in terms of changing it's current living status. An abusive relationship is included in this category as well, even if the abused partner has done the work to heal an old wound. It's what's left behind, in terms of the fear of being subjected to any manner of control or abuse again that has to be weighed in order to make a smart choice. It's important not to be influenced entirely by past experiences, but ignoring them entirely isn't appropriate either. The key is to be able to distinguish the similarities and differences between an old relationship and a current one, and to use that information to help you make an informed decision.

Someone who experienced the sting of physical or emotional abuse in a relationship may find it extremely difficult to trust again, even after having done some healing work. While trust issues left over from an abusive relationship are understandable, they limit a relationship and prevent it from moving forward. When talking about relationships, my mentor frequently opined, "Where there's no trust, there's no love." He was absolutely right. It can take quite a while before someone feels safe enough to trust another person with his or her heart again, but it's impossible to deepen intimacy without trust. I struggled with my trust issues for years, and it was only by finally resolving them that I was able to commit to my partner. One of the issues that kept repeating in previous relationships was whether or not the woman I was in relationship with was trustworthy. Over time my partner made me feel that trust was not an issue I needed to be concerned about. There are other factors that may figure into the decision whether to just continuing dating or take the relationship to the next level.

Money Matters

Financial concerns may prevent a couple from moving a relationship along the path, especially if one partner is considerably more solvent than the other. Assuming someone else's everyday living expense requires careful thought and consideration to avoid any recriminations down the road. I've observed quite a few boomer relationships in which the financial disparity between partners was pronounced. It seems like the moneyed partner's expectations, whether verbalized or not, determined the relationship's tone and ultimately even its viability.

Financial generosity has to be partnered with generosity of spirit by the partner who's supporting the relationship. The two generosities in combination represent a fully baked philosophy for the person assuming financial responsibility. Don't sell the reality of this decision short. Financial generosity absent generosity of spirit is the methodology behind how banks loan money, and the bank's expectations are made crystal clear in their voluminous documentation. That's not how couples create a future together. Generosity of spirit defines the quality of the partner's generosity.

Fred's Foundation for Lost Women

Fred was a fellow in my men's group many years ago. He'd been divorced for decades and was enormously wealthy. Unfortunately for the cavalcade of women he moved in and out of his home on a regular basis, Fred was a classic narcissist. Fred pushed women through his home's revolving door like a hotel bellman. And he showed little or no consideration for his short-term guests' well being when they found themselves at the curb with their suitcases. He simply shut the door and changed the linens for the next guest's arrival, which was as soon as he could fill the vacancy.

Worse, he consistently blamed each woman for every relationship failure, never assuming any personal responsibility. He didn't really know any of these women prior to moving them in, and in truth, they didn't really know him either. There was no basis in reality for his invitations or their acceptances. Important decisions made so casually demean the inviter, the invited, and the relationship. Fred's criterion for inviting a woman to live in his home was simple. He exclusively invited women who were in dire financial straits. He offered his home as a safe port in a storm, which to desperate women, must have felt like being given ice water in the desert. Unfortunately, his safe port was just a teaser because there were strings attached, albeit invisible ones. The strings were only hidden in the beginning; the safe port became a small boat in a stormy sea when they quickly took shape and form.

Fred controlled the tone and tenor of these financial arrangements which only vaguely resembled relationships, with an iron fist, demanding his needs be met, but rarely offering to consider the woman's. He paid for everything: food, rent, vacations, dinners out, and everything else. But his largesse never seemed to make the emotional pain that ensued bearable, because his financial generosity lacked any generosity of spirit. It was a quid pro quo for

Fred, and he expected women to pay their way in any manner that suited him.

He was abusive and mean-spirited, and sex was at his discretion. His pattern of picking desperate women who lacked alternatives included one that he married. I'd dated this woman a few times but decided not to take continue dating her because I felt she was sweet, but also very needy. She had childhood issues that were still influencing her everyday life. Fred met her through a dating service, and since I'd mentioned her at a meeting, he asked me what I thought of her. I told him she was sweet but needy, which I realize in retrospect sealed the deal for him. He loved sweet, desperate, needy women. Fred was a fan of shooting fish in a barrel.

His future wife knew his track record, and while he demanded a pre-nuptial agreement, she was guaranteed a specified sum of money for each year they remained married. Their prenuptial agreement was as thick as a small town phone book. She walked away with a bagful of bucks when they divorced a few years later, but she'd already paid a heavy price for it. Her self-esteem and dignity were trashed. As was typical for Fred, he blamed her for the failed marriage, and he was actually surprised by the level of anger when she mustered the nerve to leave him. She was so angry, in fact, that she attempted to get more than what she was owed for her services as Fred's wife. I lost touch with people who knew Fred but I heard he married again a few years later. It's hard to imagine a different outcome.

No Free Lunch

Here's what I know with absolute certainty. There's no free lunch in a restaurant or a relationship. A boomer man or woman willing to pay for everything likely has an agenda around their generosity, and it's not necessarily connected with love. The exception to this rule is the man or woman who embodies the quality commonly referred to as generosity of spirit. But with their exception, there's typically some amount of control implied when one person offers to pay all the bills. There's a hierarchy in financially lopsided relationships, and it's the man or woman at the top of the money pyramid in control. Fortunately, boomer women are in a far better financial position today than they were decades ago, and while not all boomer women are financially secure, fewer need a man to save them. It's only through generosity of spirit that a lopsided financial situation can work, because it means that the giving comes from a loving, compassionate place without any expectations.

Fred left our group because few of the men were willing to support his borderline misogynistic behavior with women, and most of us had grown weary from listening to how these ungrateful women mistreated him. For reasons I never fully understood he seemed to need the group's approval to justify his behavior with women, and with the exception of one fellow, he never got it. One particular evening after he'd told a particularly horrific story, that reflected his callous, narcissistic behavior regarding his wife's feelings, I lost control. I stood over him and shouted at the top of my lungs, "You're the most cold-hearted, selfish prick I've ever met." Fred went ballistic and insisted on immediately polling each man in the group regarding whether or not they agreed with my assessment. All but one agreed. Fred left the group, but true to form in terms of his need for approval he lobbied to get back in the group a few years later when his wife divorced him. He needed an audience for his anger and dysfunctional behavior, and although we were skeptical, a few of us met with him to see if his attitude about women had changed in the last few years. It hadn't. With the exception of the one fellow who always supported him, everyone else rejected Fred's membership. Fred served a very expensive free lunch, and he did so without a scintilla of generosity of spirit. Caveat emptor.

Other Choices

Some boomers don't feel any compelling reasons not to continue a relationship, on either a casual or exclusive dating basis, neither of which necessitates either partner moving into or out of their homes. Some boomer men and women express an overwhelming desire for the privacy and freedom that exclusive, and even casual dating can still afford, and this isn't an issue one person should ever consider persuading the other to change his or her attitude about.

While it's premature to talk about where a relationship is headed too early, there's usually some conversation about it after two people have been dating exclusively, even for a short while. A partner expressing the need to be alone most of the time isn't likely to change his or her point of view too quickly. Believing otherwise, or that you can change how that person feels, is a fantasy. Pay attention to what you hear and accept it as the other person's absolute truth, and please don't discount or ignore it.

Any decision regarding whether or not to take a relationship to the next level has to be made by both partners on a mutually agreed upon basis. And this isn't a conversation in which one partner should try to prevail over the other. It's either mutually agreeable or it just won't work. It's rare when someone is pressured to do something he or she didn't agree with that they later felt grateful. That only happens in the movies. Real life relationships don't work that way.

Living Together

Some boomers contend there's little if any difference between being married and living together. I've been in both situations and I disagree. The differences may be subtle but they matter nonetheless. Cohabitating is a euphemism for living together. In the sixties we referred to it with a slang label, shacking up, which described most of the relationships in which a couple shared an apartment or house, and usually involved one person moving into the other's place. Boomers remember a time when living together was simply considered dating on steroids. Men and women frequently made the decision to live together casually, and with little criteria beyond sex; living together didn't necessarily imply a long-term commitment. That wasn't usually the goal, and few cohabiting relationships remained faithful, meaningful or lasted.

Living together was simply an easier way to date since no one had to go home, sex was readily available, and in many ways, two actually could live cheaper than one. We were young and most of us had off the chart libidos. I can't recall anyone who actually agonized about the decision to move in with a girlfriend or boyfriend. It wasn't a serious commitment, and in retrospect sex, drugs, and rock and roll, wasn't really a viable relationship philosophy, but rather one that simply satisfied a couple's immediate needs. Few of us had well-developed emotional skills, and what's crystal clear from the thousands of comments on my sex, dating, and relationship articles, some of us still don't.

Older But Not Necessarily Wiser

We're older now and many of us have done some amount of personal growth work, which better equips us to be in successful relationships. But many boomers have ignored following any path leading to personal growth, and consequently continue behaving in the same manner they always have, which leaves them ill-prepared to relate successfully to another adult.

Most boomers recognize that the decision to cohabitate is no longer a casual one and that the criteria for living together are far more significant than they were decades ago. Avoiding rocket ride relationships is on most boomer's radar screens after feeling wounded and healing several times. Considerations such as health, retirement, family, finances, core values and beliefs, where to live, and many other critical factors require thoughtfulness and likely some compromise too. No boomer wants to screw up again. It's too emotionally jarring. Cautious optimism is warranted when considering changing your living status, which means being conscious, not cynical.

Love Means Saying You're Sorry Sometimes

The 1970 film *Love Story* stated that love means you never have to say you're sorry. That's the worst nonsense I think anyone in a movie ever uttered. Unfortunately, some boomers subscribed to this philosophy, but most just laughed when it was said onscreen. Marriage should never be considered a no-brainer, no matter the depth of love and devotion both partners feel for each other. Since marriage is a legal contract, the state gets involved in a manner many boomers remember painfully when divorcing. It's the legal unwinding of failed marriages that conjures up memories of lawyers, depositions, financial settlements, child support, property division, and more. None of these memories is sweet, and just the thought of going through this unwinding process again sends chills up most boomers' spines. In reality, that chill is our failed marriage demons taking huge bites out of our hearts. When these demons surface it can feel like it all happened yesterday instead of a decade ago or longer. That's a hard feeling to ignore.

I'm not suggesting that marriage is a mistake for boomers who divorced once or even several times. I am suggesting that it's a decision that should be made weighing factors other than just feeling in love. I met a woman recently who expressed dismay at her husband's lack of emotional skills after a few years of marriage. When I asked why she married him since it was both partners' third, all she could manage was that he made her laugh. That didn't seem like strong relationship glue.

Marriage isn't like living together on steroids any more for boomers, and hopefully a lifetime commitment will have the legs to withstand the most difficult times. Marriage is probably the biggest event a boomer will experience in his or her fifties, sixties, and beyond and the benefits and pitfalls should be transparent before making that commitment. Starry-eyed love prevents couples from being conscious and present. Boomers are smarter than that.

Health Is a New Consideration

Health is a major factor now when deciding whether or not to move forward in a relationship. It rarely even existed as an issue when boomers were in relationships decades ago, and I admit how surprised I was at first by the number of women's firmly stated comments that they're not remotely interested in getting into a relationship that would require taking care of a man with health issues. Some even expressed the prospect of being a caretaker as repellant, preferring instead to live alone for the rest of their lives. A very small number said they'd volunteer to be a caretaker for a partner with health issues in a new relationship. While men seem less likely to want to dive into this discussion, many likely feel similarly. Health issues are difficult to ignore in terms of getting into a relationship, particularly if a new partner requires a high level of care. Some of us are fortunate to enjoy good health without making too much effort, some of us were proactive and took good care of ourselves to ensure it, and some of us are simply in bad health no matter how proactive we were. No matter the causes or reasons, a partner's health requires serious consideration in a new relationship.

Sexual Health

Since most boomers are still sexually active, physical health can make the difference between good sex and none. If you have a healthy libido and embark on a new relationship with someone who is neither healthy nor has a strong libido, you're voluntarily giving up sex. While it may seem unimportant to a small number of boomers, for most it's not. I'm enjoying sex with my partner as much or more than I did when I was younger, primarily because we've worked to deepen the emotional intimacy between us, but also because we both still enjoy sex.

My boomer men and women friends are nearly all healthy and sexually active, and I doubt any would willingly give up sex if they were considering a new relationship. And if you think you'd be okay giving up sex in a new relationship, I urge you to think long and hard about what many would consider an extreme sacrifice. Sex may not be the stickiest glue to hold boomer relationships together, but it does provide an intimate activity that combines physical and emotional intimacy, and that level of physical intimacy would be difficult to duplicate in another arena.

Real Life Stuff

My partner and I are dating exclusively midway through our second year. We spend three or more nights a week together, alternating between her home and mine. Her family health history includes Alzheimer's and it's something she occasionally talks about with grave concern. I love her more than I imagined loving any woman, but I have to consider her concerns along with my own. Taking care of her should she become diagnosed with Alzheimer's would be a daunting task, but one I hope I'd be up to. I've experienced a fair amount of pain and suffering in my life, and I'm confident I'd be able rise to the occasion, because I love her more than I fear the potential for pain. But it's all conversation until it happens.

I've learned most of what I know about becoming a caretaker from my partner, who is a psychotherapist and who teaches men and women how to be caretakers for elderly relatives. She never sugar coats the reality of this monumental task, but I still consider the possibility of becoming her caretaker as the price of admission to be in a loving, sweet relationship. But I'm not wearing blinders. I've done my homework and I know what it might look like to be responsible for someone with Alzheimer's. I'm not going away because of a potential health threat some time down the road. I'm not a cut and run kind of guy anymore, and I don't abandon those I love. But it's out there in terms of a potential threat, and I can only hope my partner doesn't have to face this disease, or that a cure will be discovered before it ever becomes an issue.

Sarah and I were talking about people we'd met online in the past, and she mentioned a man she'd met online several years before. When she actually met this fellow in person she immediately noticed that he walked haltingly, and after asking about it he told her he had early-stage Parkinson's. She chose not to become involved with him, especially since his illness was already impacting his life. This is a far different choice than whether or not to take care of someone with whom you're already in a relationship. But it does force a decision regarding whether or not to become involved in a new relationship with someone who suffers from serious health issues. I didn't have any opinion about her choice because I doubt I would have dealt with the situation differently, but no one really knows what he or she might do in another person's place.

This may all sound too clinical, unfeeling and unfair, but boomers can't ignore the health aspects that are a part of choosing partners, because what feels viable today may feel untenable and regrettable later. I wish it weren't so, but it is, and that means deciding what your threshold for pain is regarding the potential for becoming a caretaker for a new partner with health issues. Whichever choice you make has consequences, albeit short-term consequences, should you decide not to become involved. No one wants to live with the sense they've treated another human being's feelings glibly. I'm not offering advice about whether or not to become involved in a relationship with someone with health issues. I'm merely suggesting that it's a decision that requires careful consideration and introspection.

How You Feel On The Inside

A more likely scenario for boomers is that a potential partner will have emotional health issues. Physical health problems that aren't life-threatening can usually be addressed if medicine is available. But a boomers' emotional health is an issue we've either chosen to face or to ignore, and someone that has chosen to ignore their emotional health brings potentially serious, risk-filled baggage into a relationship. There are medications for depression, and it seems like a substantial number of boomers are taking them. Having these drugs eliminates at least some of the mental health issues boomers face when looking for a partner.

For boomers who have done, or are doing, the work to move beyond the limitations emotional health issues have presented, getting involved with a partner that hasn't or isn't, can feel like being stuck between a rock and a hard place. Not wanting or liking to talk about one's feelings in a relationship is problematic, but workable. Not knowing how to talk about one's feelings is an entirely different matter, because it presents a dead end every time trouble appears. There's simply no place for a relationship to go to work out problems unless both partners know how to talk about issues as they arise, and this skillset isn't second-nature to many people.

Looking in the mirror can make boomers feel as if their time to find a partner is limited, which, while partially true, can create an unbearable feeling of pressure. But putting one's head in the sand about a potential partner's emotional health will most certainly have repercussions. My partner and I have done a fair amount of emotional work, and we still have issues that we struggle with at times. What makes our relationship work is that we both have the skills to talk these issues out based on what we've learned about ourselves over the years. Sometimes there's an initial outburst, and some amount of angry back and forth before we manage to focus on the problem. When that occurs we try to create a quiet, safe space that allows us to talk through the issue in terms of our feelings about it, not our thoughts.

I grimace when I recall how I functioned, or actually, didn't function, in relationships in the years before I faced my demons. I was a nightmare for many women, and what made it worse was few of my ex-girlfriends had the requisite skills either. Most of those old relationships ended with a flare-up that quickly became a raging inferno. I was too myopic to see the point of sifting through the ashes afterward to glean my part in the fiasco.

Many boomers are in therapy or doing some modality of personal growth work with the intention of discarding old baggage. Depending how far along we are on this path this is a positive sign. While someone who's just begun doing their work may still be too raw, in terms of being immediate relationship material, someone who has been doing personal growth work for a while, indicates a person with a strong interest in getting it right in their life.

Love At First Sight Is Totally Blind

I knew a boomer woman who met a man on a flight from Los Angeles to New York, and by the time their plane landed they'd already decided to get married the next day. Predictably, the marriage lasted two weeks. Of course this is extreme behavior that represents an absolute absence of conscious thought. But I've known a fair number of boomers who have married for reasons that were unclear to them at the time or that they couldn't articulate. Some of the reasons offered were pity, infatuation, loneliness, desperation, and a lack of respect for marriage as a long-term commitment.

I'm a big fan of marriage when it's a conscious commitment, and while it's still too soon for my partner and me to engage in serious conversation about it, we share the desire to be together in some manner in the future. It may be cohabitating or marriage, and while I'm not a betting guy I'd say the odds are good that we'll succeed at whichever we choose, and for all the important reasons I've mentioned in this chapter.

Conclusion

You have all the tools you need to begin your online dating journey, and I sincerely hope that this information will yield the results you desire. I realize how discouraging it can feel to have a string of dates with people you met online, only to have them all fall flat.

It took me nearly two years to meet my partner but it was well worth the wait. Perhaps your life partner will show up sooner. When you become frustrated, weary, or simply lose interest in the online dating process, take a break and come back to it when you're feeling positive again.

Your life partner is out there, and he or she is looking for you with the same intensity and desire, so don't give up. It's just a matter of your two worlds colliding.

Good luck.

Ken

Made in the USA
San Bernardino, CA
23 March 2015